Open for Debate

Terrorism

Open for Debate

Terrorism

Lila Perl

BENCHMARK BOOKS

MARSHALL CAVENDISH
NEW YORK

Thanks to Dr. Bruce Hoffman,
director of the RAND corporation,
for his expert reading of this manuscript.

Benchmark Books
Marshall Cavendish
99 White Plains Road
Tarrytown, New York 10591-9001
www.marshallcavendish.com

Library of Congress Cataloging-in-Publication Data
Perl, Lila.
Terrorism / by Lila Perl.
p. cm.--(Open for debate)
Summary: Defines and discusses the history of terrorism,
the nature of terrorism and terrorists, and the recent,
rapid growth of terrorist acts throughout the world.
Includes bibliographical references and index.
ISBN 0-7614-1583-1
1. Terrorism—Juvenile literature. 2. Terrorists—Juvenile literature.
[1. Terrorism. 2. Terrorists.] I. Title. II. Series.
HV6431.P464 2003
303.6'25—dc21
2002155976

Photo research by Linda Sykes Picture Research, Inc., Hilton Head, SC

The photographs in this book are used by permission and through the courtesy of:
© 2001 Getty Images: Cover, 2–3, 6, 16, 127; Topical Press/Getty Images: 28, 37, 64;
AP/Wide World Photos: 30, 53, 85, 97, 114; Keystone/Getty Images: 71; Express/Getty
Images: 93; Al Rai Al Aam/Feature Story News/Liaison/Getty Images: 108.

Series design by Sonia Chaghatzbanian

Printed in China

1   3   5   6   4   2

Contents

THE terrorists of SEPTEMBER 11, 2001, crashed an airliner into the
PENTAGON in ARLINGTON, VIRGINIA, tearing a 200-foot (61-M) gash into

U.S. ATTACKED

HIJACKED JETS DESTROY TWIN TOWERS AND HIT PENTAGON IN DAY OF TERROR

These were the headlines in *The New York Times* on the morning after the shocking and harrowing events of September 11, 2001.

Tuesday, September 11, dawned pleasant and sunny in New York City and along the eastern seaboard of the United States. The flying weather was excellent and the air traffic was relatively light because it was a Tuesday, typically one of the slower travel days of the week. Two morning flights departed routinely from Boston's Logan

Airport, carrying business travelers, vacationers, and other civilians going cross-country for a variety of personal reasons.

The first of the two takeoffs was American Airlines Flight 11, a Boeing 767 bound for Los Angeles. At 8:46 A.M., less than an hour after it had become airborne, horrified onlookers saw Flight 11 crash into the North Tower of New York City's World Trade Center, striking the 110-story building somewhere between the ninety-fourth and ninety-eighth floors.

Black smoke immediately billowed from the topmost floors of the building. The plane had been fully loaded with jet fuel for its nearly 3,000-mile (4,828-km) flight, and the flames that ensued may have been as hot as 2000 degrees Fahrenheit (1093 °C). Onlookers with long memories and people familiar with aviation disasters wondered if an appalling accident had taken place. On July 28, 1945, while World War II was still in progress in the Pacific, a B-25 bomber had accidentally flown into New York City's Empire State Building during a thick fog. Remarkably, however, the flash fire that broke out between the seventy-eighth and seventy-ninth floors was put out within thirty-five minutes and did limited damage to the building. The bomber carried only 800 gallons (3,027 l) of gasoline as opposed to Flight 11's 10,000 gallons (37,843 l) of jet fuel. Nor was the Empire State's death toll of fourteen people as high as had been feared at the time of impact.

In the case of the North Tower, which bore the address One World Trade Center, it quickly became evident that a major catastrophe was taking place. People on the ground began to observe a horrifying sight. Figures of human beings, fleeing the searing heat and choking smoke of the burning jet fuel, began to leap and drop from the upper floors of the building. Bodies of men and women, mainly office workers and building staff, came tumbling toward the ground. Figures twisted helplessly during the hundreds of feet of free fall. An eyewitness told *Newsweek* reporter Jerry Adler that "jumpers landed with such force that a pink mist of gore rose from the sidewalk as they hit."

Proof that the crashing of a jet plane into one of the Twin Towers was no accident came almost immediately. Within seventeen minutes, at 9:03 A.M., the second take-off from Boston's Logan Airport—United Airlines Flight 175, also a Boeing 767 and also bound for Los Angeles—was seen to head directly into the South Tower, known as Two World Trade Center. The plane struck between the seventy-eighth and eighty-fourth stories, lower than on the first tower. The impact instantly enveloped the upper third of the building in an enormous billow of brilliant orange flame. Less than one hour later, just short of 10 A.M., the South Tower began to collapse. It neither swayed nor fell over. It simply imploded, or burst inward, its steel supports giving way in the intense heat, its columns buckling, and its floors pancaking one atop the other in a chain reaction.

Half an hour later, at 10:29 A.M., the first-hit North Tower collapsed in similar fashion. It became a mountainous smoking ruin of dust and rubble, consisting of pulverized concrete, huge shards of structural steel, shattered glass, marble, wallboard, gypsum, office equipment, electrical cables, restroom sinks and toilets, and whirling sheets of paper. The paper and similarly airborne contents of desks and filing cabinets would soon cover a radius of miles.

Unseen beneath the rubble of the collapsed towers were the several underground levels that contained concourses of shops and eateries, subway stations, and parking garages for more than 600 vehicles. The World Trade Center complex also included a number of other buildings, some of which either also collapsed or were so seriously damaged as to become hazardous. Approximately 50,000 people were believed to work or to have been present at the site when the fires first broke out. How many could have survived?

New York City was still reeling from what appeared to be a terrorist attack of the greatest magnitude when it was learned that a Boeing 757—American Airlines Flight 77 out of Washington, D.C.'s Dulles Airport bound for Los Angeles—had changed course and slammed into the Pentagon. The nation's military headquarters was hit at 9:37 A.M. One portion of the five-sided, five-story concrete structure was badly damaged by an explosion and fire. The attackers had almost certainly hoped to demolish more of the fifty-eight-year-old building, which at that time employed 24,000 persons, including the highest echelons of U.S. military personnel.

A fourth plane, it was learned, had also been hijacked on the morning of September 11. United Airlines Flight 93—another Boeing 757—flew out of Newark bound for San Francisco, with the possible intention of changing course and heading for a target such as the White House or the Capitol Building. Flight 93, however, crashed in a Pennsylvania field, 80 miles (129 km) southeast of Pittsburgh. Messages received via cellular telephone from passengers on that aircraft, and on others used in the coordinated attack, clearly indicated that terrorists aboard had taken over the flights and directed or attempted to direct them to their intended targets. It was soon learned that 246 passengers and crew had perished on the four airplanes, as well as nineteen hijackers.

Nobody knew yet how many had been killed on the ground, but early estimates ran as high as 20,000, later amended to 5,000 or 6,000. Nor had anyone yet claimed responsibility for the worst terrorist attack on American soil in the nation's history. Certain to be high on the list of suspects, however, was the Islamic militant leader Osama bin Laden, at that time resident in Afghanistan, mastermind of the Al Qaeda terror network, and deliverer of anti-American threats and attacks on American targets since the early 1990s.

1
A Growing Menace

Terrorism is as recent as the September 11, 2001, attack on the World Trade Center and the Pentagon and as old as the history of humankind. It is also surprisingly difficult to define. It involves violent acts as crude and unsophisticated as throwing stones to destroy property and harm people, and as savage and ruthless as turning an airplane full of innocent people into a flying bomb.

How can we say what terrorism is and how can we separate it from other forms of criminal behavior? The U.S. Federal Bureau of Investigation (FBI) defines terrorism as "the unlawful use of force or violence against persons or property to intimidate or coerce a government, the civilian population, or any segment thereof, in furtherance of political or social objectives."

Osama bin Laden, confirmed to have been the mastermind of the September 11 attack, traced his terrorist roots to a secret Islamic society of the eleventh to thirteenth centuries, known as the Assassins. The word assassin comes from the Arabic *hashshash*, meaning one addicted to hashish, for during the time of the Crusades it was the practice of this group to terrorize and murder Christians and other enemies while under the influence of a narcotic. Bin Laden, whose political objective appeared to be the ousting of Americans from the Islamic nations of the world and the murder of Americans on their own soil, may well have modeled himself on Hasan-e Sabbah, the founder of the Assassins. The followers of the Assassins' leader, also known to the Crusaders as the Old Man of the Mountains, roamed the Middle East from Persia (now Iran) to Syria.

Intimidation, the creation of a climate of fear, like that which resulted from the September 11 attack, is one of the goals of terrorism. The victims, whether an entire nation or a portion of its citizenry, no longer feel that their government can protect them. The effects of a terrorist act and the anticipation that others will follow make normal life impossible.

Unlawfulness, or illegality, is another characteristic of terrorism. The word "terrorism" was first used in the late 1700s during the French Revolution. After seizing power, the revolutionaries set up a "reign of terror" that claimed many lives from all levels of society and, finally, even that of their fanatical leader Robespierre. Yet, the executions by guillotine and other means were sanctioned by the government of France at that time. Technically, a government's oppression of its own people does not fit the modern definition of terrorism.

Similarly, the genocide—ethnic and racial killing—practiced in Hitler's Germany and in the lands the Nazis overran during World War II, monstrous as it was, was carried out by a duly elected government that subsequently embarked on a war of conquest. Murderous regimes like that of Fascist Italy under Mussolini and the Soviet Union under Stalin certainly practiced terror. But their tyrant leaders were also heads of state. As a result, such criminals do not meet the criterion of having committed "unlawful" acts under the FBI definition of terrorism. To widen the definition or use the term more loosely would take the survey at hand into the most distant and broadest reaches of human history.

Terrorism, as it is currently understood, does not apply to acts of war either. Overwhelmed by both the surprise element and the large expected death toll of the September 11 attack, Americans found themselves comparing it to Pearl Harbor. Although the Japanese attack on the United States naval base on December 7, 1941, resulted in nearly 2,400 deaths—including some civilians—and extensive damage to Americans warships and to aircraft on the ground, it was an act of war rather than one of terrorism. A military conflict was already raging in Europe and Asia, and the target was military rather than civilian. Also, the Hawaiian island of Oahu lay at a great distance from the United States mainland.

Foreign incursions on American soil had otherwise been rare. Nothing had so shaken the nation as the events of September 11, 2001. Ordinary people going on with their lives—flying in an airplane, walking to work in a Lower Manhattan office building, riding in an elevator, sitting at a desk—were suddenly faced with death at the hands of an unknowable, uncontrollable, overpowering force.

Although terrorism can be differentiated from war in the conventional sense, it is nevertheless a form of warfare. It is also, all too often, planned and deliberate murder.

Sometimes terrorism is, or appears to be, the work of crazy people, malcontents, or misfits, who have no clear-cut social or political goal. But most of the time this form of violence is carried out by men and women determined to bring about some form of social or political change.

The terrorists who carried out the September 11 attack were violently against the presence of Americans in Muslim lands and wanted to send a warning to Americans that they were at risk even on their own soil. The terrorists' actions were rooted in such strong religious beliefs that they were willing to undertake suicide missions in order to kill as many Americans as possible. Like the Assassins of the eleventh century, who had conducted suicide raids on enemy fortresses in the Middle East, the September 11 attackers had taken the pledge to give up their lives in order to destroy the perceived enemy.

It was learned that nineteen hijackers recruited from various parts of the Muslim world had distributed themselves among the four airplanes. Shortly after the planes were airborne, the terrorists had subdued the passengers and crew, using small weapons that they had smuggled aboard. Some of the hijackers, who had enrolled in flight schools in the United States, invaded the cockpits and took control of the aircraft, which they then steered into the selected targets.

In the history of terrorism, not all religious extremists have undertaken suicidal missions. Yet, in recent decades, such missions have been increasing in number. Among Muslims, there is disagreement as to whether religious warriors are permitted to take their own lives.

The Koran, the holy book of Islam, which contains the writings of the prophet Muhammad as revealed to him by

THE FIRST PLANE STRUCK THE NORTH TOWER AT 8:46 A.M. AND WAS FOLLOWED BY
A SECOND, WHICH HIT THE SOUTH TOWER AT 9:03 A.M.

God, or Allah, prohibits suicide. Yet, Islamic militants do not see certain forms of self-destruction, such as martyrdom, as suicide. They maintain that the Palestinian Muslim youth who blows himself up along with Israeli citizens on a bus or a busy street in Tel Aviv or Jerusalem is a hero of the faith. Likewise, the more sophisticated Islamic terrorist who rams an airplane full of passengers into a New York City skyscraper is seen as performing a sacred duty.

Islamic militants believe that the act of giving one's life for jihad, which is defined as "struggle," and, in terms of the religion as "holy war," guarantees rewards in the hereafter. Successful suicide bombers are assured that they will immediately enter Paradise, a heavenly garden that is reserved for prophets and martyrs. There, the sins of he who has sacrificed his life will be washed away at once. He will face no reckoning on the Day of Judgment, and on the Day of Resurrection he will be allowed to intercede for the salvation of seventy of his nearest and dearest family members. In Paradise, he will enjoy the company of seventy-two young maidens. By tradition, only males have been seen as candidates to wage jihad.

A number of factors make terrorism a growing menace in the age of the suicide bomber. The success of the September 11 attack on the United States can be traced to two unfortunate circumstances. One was the commitment and careful planning of the terrorists. The other was the complacency and lack of coordination among the intelligence-gathering and other security agencies in the United States.

Who were the terrorists that Osama bin Laden recruited for the brazen attack on the citizens and landmarks of the United States, and how did they proceed with their deadly business?

"Attackers Believed to Be Sane"

In an attempt to analyze the mindset of the nineteen hijackers, Erica Goode wrote in *The New York Times* on September 12, 2001, that these members of the Al Qaeda group appeared to be "not depressed, just indoctrinated in their cause."

Goode reported that

Studies suggest that those willing to sacrifice their lives in an attack are almost never the disturbed loners sometimes conjured by the news media or by Hollywood films. Instead they are almost always part of a larger organization that has recruited them, tested their courage and trained them to carry out their missions with precision.

Goode quoted Dr. Harvey W. Kushner, an expert in terrorism and chairman of the department of criminal justice at Long Island University. Dr. Kushner noted that suicide attacks are not condoned by most Muslims, but are espoused "by leaders of religious factions within the Islamic community" who have what he described as "a contorted view of what is spiritually permissible. . . . The person who does this does not see himself as giving up his life at a premature point. He sees it as for the greater good of society. And for us to try to guard against this, it's disastrous."

Marwan al-Shehhi wrote: "Remember to pray before reaching the target. After that, God willing, we will meet in Paradise." Mohamed Atta wrote: "When the hour of reality, the zero hour, approaches, open your heart and welcome death for the sake of God."

Probably the greatest failure of immigration, security, and police officials in allowing the terrorists free reign on American soil was their inefficiency and lack of imagination. The nation and its authorities were caught by surprise on September 11. No one was truly prepared for a destructive act of such immense proportions. And not many could understand the thinking of the nineteen men who approached death with such determination and joy.

The ringleader of the nineteen terrorists appeared to have been Mohamed Atta, a university-educated Egyptian in his early thirties. He was the only son of a Cairo lawyer and a doting mother, and had two older sisters who were university professors. He did not fit the picture of a poor youth without a future, one who might blow himself up to enter the Gates of Paradise.

After graduating from Cairo University, Atta pursued an advanced degree in urban planning at a university in Hamburg, Germany. He left Egypt, in part, because he violently disagreed with his government's friendly relationship with the United States, its accords with Israel, and its imprisonment of Islamic fundamentalists like himself.

In Hamburg, the deeply religious Atta frequented a mosque that was attended by other Islamic extremists living in the city. Soon he made contact with the Al Qaeda terror organization of Osama bin Laden, headquartered in Afghanistan, and went there for a year to receive training in one of its camps. On his return to Hamburg in 1998, he became the leader of a terrorist cell in an apartment that was outfitted with computers and high-speed phone lines. His closest companions were Marwan al-Shehhi, the son of an imam, or Muslim prayer leader, from the United Arab Emirates, and Ziad Samir al-Jarrah, a Lebanese from a well-to-do family, who was studying aeronautical engineering and dreamed of becoming a pilot. They, too, had been to Afghanistan for terrorist training.

Late in 1999, in preparation for their first infiltration of the United States, all three reported their passports stolen and received new ones that showed no record of their ever having been in Afghanistan. In the summer of 2000, they obtained tourist visas. Traveling separately, they arrived in the United

States on flights from Berlin. Although Germany was known to host communities of Muslims, some of whom were students from Middle Eastern nations, the United States immigration authorities saw no reason to deny the visas.

Atta and his companions immediately established themselves in Florida for the purpose of enrolling in flight school. Although they did not have the student visas required for foreign-born nationals who want to study in the United States, the school accepted them when they paid the necessary fees. Throughout their stay in America, the terrorists were provided with funds through an Al Qaeda intermediary working out of the United Arab Emirates.

After completing their training in flying light aircraft, the terrorists went on to receive jet-simulator training. They were not interested in learning takeoffs and landings. Their stated purpose was to learn how to steer a jet airplane.

During the time they spent in Florida, the terrorists managed to blend in successfully with the population. They shaved the beards that were required by religious law, were careful never to pray in public, and dressed in Western clothes. They rented apartments and cars without giving vital information about their backgrounds, and they used computers in commercial facilities so that their messages could not be traced.

Nevertheless, they did have brushes with the law in Florida. One of them received a traffic ticket but never appeared in court and was not pursued by the authorities. During their light-plane training, the terrorists stalled a small plane on the runway of Miami International Airport in December 2000 and left it there. The Federal Aviation Agency never followed up on this serious offense.

As the time for the September 11 attack drew closer,

the other members of the team arrived. All had originally trained at Al Qaeda camps in Afghanistan. Fifteen of the nineteen hijackers would turn out to be Saudi Arabians. Some enrolled in Florida gyms to take martial arts training, stressing aggressive tactics for use in close quarters. Their job would be to subdue the passengers and crew in hand-to-hand contact. Other team members arrived on July 4, 2001, and joined a cell that had already been set up in an apartment in Paterson, New Jersey.

Mohamed Atta visited the group in New Jersey. Especially brazen, however, were trips he made to Europe in the months before the attack, probably to meet with fellow terrorists. Each time he returned to the United States, immigration officials issued him a tourist visa, even though he had overstayed the time limit on his first tourist visa.

As September 11 approached, the hijackers made test runs by purchasing tickets for the very flights that they would later hijack. They also practiced getting box cutters and knives past the airport security guards, which they accomplished with no difficulty.

In the twenty-four hours before September 11, the terrorists sent the money they would not need back to the Al Qaeda agent working out of the United Arab Emirates. These funds could then be used toward future missions. The amount of money the group had received, in small increments, during its preparations in the United States, was calculated to be $500,000, actually a very small sum in view of the numerous lives lost and the magnitude of the damage.

On the eve of September 11, Mohamed Atta and a fellow terrorist flew to Portland, Maine, and from there to Boston for the planned attacks. Atta boarded American Airlines Flight 11, the plane that he would crash into the

North Tower of the World Trade Center. Al-Shehhi followed him on United Airlines Flight 175, which destroyed the South Tower.

Both men left writings attesting to their resolve to die for their religious beliefs.

2
The Ku Klux Klan

Are terrorists living among us? This was the question that Americans began asking themselves in the weeks and months following the attack of September 11. The suicide bombers, the public soon learned, had been living in their communities, shopping in their stores, had even been their neighbors in the same apartment building or housing complex.

How many more potential killers had the attackers left behind for the next terrorist operation? Americans wondered. It was also soon learned that it was the practice of international terrorist groups to plant agents known as sleepers in the target country. Their purpose was to remain in place, living quietly among the general population, until they were called upon for a new mission of violence.

In the aftermath of September 11, few Americans thought to look back on a prolonged period of terror and violence that had been visited regularly on targets in the

United States, not by foreign extremists but by their own countrymen and women.

For more than a hundred years, immediately following the end of the Civil War in 1865, white supremacists who had organized into a secret society known as the Ku Klux Klan operated a terror network on American soil. Disguising their identity in pointed white hoods and long white robes, its members were responsible for the deaths of thousands of people, most of them African Americans.

The Klan was born in a small Tennessee town on the Alabama border around December 1865. Its first members were a group of six Confederate veterans who had served in the armies of the defeated South. Their leader was Confederate General Nathan Bedford Forrest, who was elected Grand Wizard. The Klan took its name from *kuklos*, the Greek word for circle, and like many secret societies it chose fanciful titles for its subdivisions and their members. Within the Klan "Empire," there were units headed by Grand Dragons, Titans, Giants, and Cyclopses.

There was nothing playful, however, about the purpose of the newly formed Klan. True to the nature of a terrorist organization, its goal was to bring about social and political change. The South was reeling from the loss of life and the destruction of property wrought by the armies of the victorious North. But even more deeply resented by much of the white population of the South was the liberation of the black slaves. After centuries of mastery over blacks, whites could not accept them as social, economic, or political equals. The Klan undertook to reverse the new order and to regain the prewar dominant status of the southern white population.

The newly freed blacks were easily frightened by the advent of the Klansmen, who proudly boasted of being "a rough bunch of boys." Soon the Klan had become active in at least nine southern states, where attacks on African Americans ranged from floggings and mutilations to death by beating, shooting, and especially by hanging. The Klan favored lynching because bodies left dangling from tree limbs were intended to set an example for others and to inculcate terror throughout the district in which the local Klan unit operated.

The African-American victims were accused of crimes ranging from mere disrespect toward whites to theft, murder, and rape. The safety and security of white womanhood in the South were regarded as threatened by the newly liberated African-American male population. The slightest whisper of improper behavior by a black man toward a white woman meant almost immediate apprehension and punishment.

Northerners who had come south after the war, especially those involved in reintegrating the seceded states into the Union, were hated and threatened by the Klan. Assisting the freedmen to obtain basic needs such as food, clothing, shelter, some abandoned land they could farm, schools for their children, voting, and other legal rights, brought on the wrath of the white-hooded riders who chose to make most of their forays at night. So whites, too, became potential victims if they believed in racial equality.

Nathan Bedford Forrest, now known as the Klan's Imperial Wizard, tried to control the violence, but was unsuccessful. As a result, he resigned in 1869 and suggested that all of the Klan's papers and other evidence be burned. The Klan's activities did not abate, however, and by the early 1870s the Klan had half a million members, distributed among numerous local units known as Klaverns. Some of the Klaverns had become rabid in their efforts to destroy freedom and rights of African Americans—through looting, torture, burning, and bloody assaults on individuals and groups.

The Klan continued to be active until 1877, when the Republicans, the party of Abraham Lincoln, ceded power in the South to the white Southern Democrats. Once the Democrats, who had favored the Confederacy, were back in control, they took over the Klan's role of bringing pressure to restore segregation and white supremacy.

The Klan, however, did not remain dormant. It was revived early in the twentieth century under the leadership of Alabama-born William J. Simmons, whose father had been a Klansman back in the 1860s. Simmons's success was due in part to the role played by Thomas Watson, U.S. congressman from Georgia, in the sensational Leo Frank case of 1913. Mary Phagan, a thirteen-year-old Christian white girl who worked in an Atlanta factory managed by Leo Max Frank, a northerner and a Jew, was found raped and murdered on April 7, 1913.

Frank, who, it was learned many years later, was innocent of the crime, was convicted and sentenced to death. When the governor of Georgia commuted Frank's sentence to life imprisonment because the evidence against him was so unconvincing, Watson launched such a fierce anti-Semitic campaign against Frank that, on August 16, 1915, a mob broke into the state prison, dragged Frank out of his cell, and lynched him.

Watson's call for a "Gentile League" to combat the Jewish presence in the South, and his rallying of a lynch mob in the Frank case, inspired Simmons to bring about a rebirth of the Klan. On a November night in 1915, Simmons shepherded fifteen supporters up to the top of Stone Mountain, a huge granite outcropping located 16 miles (26 km) outside Atlanta. There he burned an enormous excelsior-padded wooden cross that had been doused with kerosene and proclaimed that "Under a blazing, fiery torch the Invisible Empire was called from its slumber . . ."

Although the stated goals of the reborn Klan were "a new mission for humanity's good," and "fraternity among men," its true purpose was to attract members who were anti-African Amercan, anti-Jewish, anti-Catholic, and anti-immigrant. Klansmen had to be "100 percent American and no other."

Simmons, who had been a traveling salesman and a fundamentalist preacher in backwoods Georgia, became the Imperial Wizard of the new Klan. Membership expanded rapidly as automobiles replaced horses in the Klan's customary night raids and increased the amount of territory its terrorist members could cover. As African Americans fled the South to work on assembly lines in the industrial Midwest, doing the same jobs as whites, the Klan followed

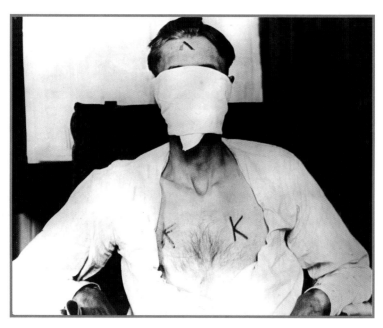

IN 1924, NELSON BURROUGHS, A WHITE CATHOLIC, WAS BRANDED WITH HOT IRONS BY THE KU KLUX KLAN BECAUSE HE REFUSED TO RENOUNCE HIS RELIGION.

them. "Blacks," Simmons decreed, "should be shipped back to Africa."

As to the Jew, Simmons declared that he had "shut himself out of the Klan" because he did not accept Jesus Christ who, according to Simmons, was the Klan's leader. Catholics were also denied admission to the Klan because of Protestant opposition to the Pope. Caleb A. Ridley, pastor of Atlanta's Central Baptist Church, and the Klan's national chaplain, with the title of Imperial Kludd, said that he could not be dictated to in politics or religion by a Pope "on the other side of the world."

Throughout the 1920s, stealthily supported by local officials, the Klan continued its lawless attacks on African Americans and their presumed white sympathizers. An African-American Pullman porter was lynched for reportedly having insulted a white female passenger traveling in the railroad car to which he was assigned. A white barber in Atlanta was accused of cutting a white man's hair with the same scissors he had used on a member of the "inferior race." He was stretched between two trees and beaten with a cleated belt until he died of his wounds.

During the Great Depression of the 1930s, the Klan lost both membership and financial strength, and attempted to renew its power by allying itself with the German American Bund, an organization directly linked to Adolf Hitler's Nazi Party in Germany. America's entry into the war against Germany in 1941, plus a bill from the U.S. Internal Revenue Service for $685,000 in back taxes (as a fraternal organization, not a criminal one), again laid the Klan temporarily to rest.

Soon its once-powerful terror network consisted of relatively few Klaverns, scattered through the backcountry of the South. Nonetheless, the Klan's "achievements" between 1880 and 1940 had been considerable. During that period,

IN 1939, WHITE-ROBED AND HOODED MEMBERS OF THE KU KLUX KLAN BURNED A FIFTEEN-FOOT CROSS—THE SYMBOL OF THEIR WHITE SUPREMACIST BELIEFS—IN TAMPA, FLORIDA.

the Klan's murders had included the lynching of almost 5,000 African Americans in the American South.

In the aftermath of World War II, a strong, new federal movement for civil-rights reform got under way, beginning with the 1954 Supreme Court decision calling for public-school desegregation. The notion that white and African-American children in the South should attend the same schools gave the Klan a reason to spring back into action. In addition to burning and shooting up African-American homes and churches, the reborn Klan now added bombings to its terror attacks. Emerging African-American leaders like the Reverend Martin Luther King

Jr. were targeted. In 1956, King's home in Montgomery, Alabama, was bombed.

The 1960s ushered in sit-ins at formerly all-white lunch counters, where African Americans attempted to assert their right to be served. The struggle for equality in other public places and for the exercise of African-American voting rights brought interracial groups of civil-rights activists from the North. The Klan responded with increased violence, and it was all too often aided and abetted by local authorities in direct violation of federal laws.

On Sunday morning, September 15, 1963, four members of the local Klan blew up the Sixteenth Street Baptist Church in Birmingham, Alabama, which was a gathering place for civil-rights demonstrators. Four young African-American girls, aged eleven to fourteen, who were attending Sunday school in the church basement, were killed. Dozens of others were injured. Although the four suspected bombers were arrested within days, the case remained inactive for many years because Alabama juries, which were composed solely of whites, were unlikely to convict a member of their own race.

The following summer, a group calling itself the White Knights of the Ku Klux Klan directly targeted civil-rights workers in Mississippi. Its victims were two young white men, Michael Schwerner and Andrew Goodman—both from New York and both Jews—and James Chaney, an African-American resident of Meridian, Mississippi, and a local civil-rights volunteer. All three were members of the Congress of Racial Equality (CORE).

On June 21, 1964, as the three were driving on a back-country road after visiting the remains of a burned-out African-American church, they were arrested by the local deputy sheriff on a charge of speeding, and were put in jail. When Schwerner, Goodman, and Chaney were released later that night, they were followed by the deputy and halted by a group of Klansmen who lay in wait for them.

Dragged out of their station wagon, they were taken to a lonely place on the road and shot dead, execution style. Their bodies, which were buried in the mud of an earthen dam where a pond was being constructed, were not found for forty-four days.

Although twenty-one men were arrested for conspiracy to murder the three civil-rights workers, it was once again impossible to get a Southern jury to convict on either the local or the state level. It took three years, until 1967, for the federal government to bring charges and for a trial to be held in the state of Mississippi. By that time, three of the Klansmen had confessed. The white jury sent the local Klan Wizard, the sheriff's deputy, and five other Klansmen to prison for terms of three to ten years, with the opportunity for earlier release through parole. The sentence appeared to be a less than adequate response to the crime of a premeditated triple murder.

In the Birmingham, Alabama, church bombing case of 1963, the Klan terrorists received even more delayed treatment. Of the four conspirators, one did not go to prison until 1977, dying there eight years later. A second died in 1994 without ever being charged. The third and fourth Klansmen, Thomas E. Blanton Jr. and Bobby Frank Cherry, were not indicted on murder charges until May 2000. Blanton was finally sent to prison in 2001, while Cherry's court date was put off until 2002 because his mental competency to stand trial was in question. Cherry, who was in his seventies, pleaded that he had a poor memory.

On May 22, 2002, however, the last of the Birmingham

"Hate, American Style"

Members of white supremacist groups in America like the KKK, who were often thought of as pillars of society, may not have looked liked today's Arab or Muslim terrorists. They may not have been willing to die for their cause, and their criminal activities may have had the support of local police and even city or state officials. But they were, and still are, America's Al Qaeda.

Nicholas D. Kristof wrote in *The New York Times* on August 30, 2002, about his recent interview with Rev. Matt Hale, the thirty-one-year-old hatemonger and leader of the World Church of the Creator, "whose followers have shot, knifed, or beaten blacks, Jews, and Asian Americans in several states."

Kristof said that though these American religious extremists are not "a threat to national stability, the way they are in Pakistan and Saudi Arabia . . . they are every bit as loony as Al Qaeda and they have been enmeshed in violence." The World Church is "an international organization with members in forty-nine states and twenty-eight countries. It claims 70,000 to 80,000 adherents and boasts in press releases that it is 'the fastest-growing white racist and anti-Semitic church in America.'"

In conducting a "racial holy war on behalf of whites," Hale's World Church of the Creator "runs a sophisticated Web site with information on, for example, how to make your own plastic explosives. The church even has a Web page for kids."

In drawing comparisons between the hate crimes committed by America's racial and religious extremists, past and present, and those of foreign groups in the name of Islamic fundamentalism, it is clear that both represent terrorist crimes. As Kristof puts it, America's hatemongers are "domestic counterparts to Islam's manic mullahs [religious leaders]."

church bombers was sentenced to life in prison by a jury of nine whites and three blacks in the state of Alabama. Bobby Frank Cherry's conviction had taken nearly forty years.

Although the days have passed when juries in the South were all white and could be counted on not to convict members of the Klan, racial, ethnic, and other hate crimes are still committed in the United States with alarming frequency. Nor have white supremacist groups disappeared from the national scene.

Today's media, especially sites on the Internet, offer information about a variety of such organizations. The Web site of The Knights, "America's Oldest, Largest, Most Professional White Rights Party" urges: "It's time for Whites to stick together" because "taking back America" is the only way to "regain control of our destiny . . . our inheritance." The Knights, based in Harrison, Arkansas, is clearly an affiliate of the KKK. Thinly veiled messages are offered concerning "the truth about Kwanzaa" and "about Martin Luther King Jr." Members are warned that while "Black people are united, White people are not."

As Americans searched the skies after September 11 for the very real threat of terrorists from abroad, they could not afford to ignore the lingering influence of the Ku Klux Klan.

3
The Irish Rebellion

Terrorism may derive from racial hatred and white supremacist beliefs, as demonstrated by the long history of the Ku Klux Klan and similar groups born and bred on American soil. Terrorism may be driven by religious extremism, as in the case of the deadly attacks on New York City and Washington, D.C., on September 11, 2001. Terrorism may also arise from the desire of an ethnic or religious group to break away from the nation of which it is a part and to establish home rule, self-government, or a completely independent nation.

The struggle for Irish independence from Great Britain represents one of the oldest nationalist movements in modern history. It had its roots in very early ethnic and religious differences. In 1534, the English king Henry VIII broke with the Roman Catholic Church, replacing it with the (Protestant) Church of England. While Henry's Irish subjects clung to the Roman Catholic faith, Protestant England continued to dominate Ireland's economy, relegating its people to poverty and helplessness.

After centuries of oppression, a series of Irish rebellions, in the form of guerrilla warfare, led to partial success. In 1922 a dominion within the British Commonwealth known as the Irish Free State was established. It consisted of the twenty-six most southerly and westerly counties of Ireland, all of which were predominantly Catholic. The six counties of northeastern Ireland, however, presented a problem. Nearly two-thirds of their population was made up of Scottish and English Protestants, known as the Scotch-Irish. This portion of Ireland, which became known as Northern Ireland, chose to remain under the direct rule of Great Britain, despite the presence of an unhappy Catholic minority.

In 1949, the Irish Free State acquired total freedom from Britain and subsequently became known as the Republic of Ireland. But in Northern Ireland, which remained part of Britain, the Catholic population had developed a festering resentment toward the Protestant majority and toward the presence of British governing bodies and British troops on Irish soil.

The Irish Republican Army (IRA), which was founded in 1919 to fight against British rule in Ireland, grew increasingly violent in the 1960s, a time when national liberation movements were springing up all over the world. In 1969, a disagreement within the IRA developed with regard to the use of terrorist tactics. As a result, a group known as the Provisional Irish Republican Army (PIRA), or the Provos, became the activist successor of the official IRA.

The enmity between Catholics and Protestants in Northern Ireland has been explained as a religious struggle only in part. It was also seen as a struggle between the un-

ARMED MEMBERS OF THE IRISH REPUBLICAN ARMY MARCH THROUGH THE STREETS OF DUBLIN IN 1922 IN OPPOSITION TO THE TREATY THAT WOULD SEPARATE NORTHERN IRELAND FROM THE IRISH FREE STATE.

derprivileged and the privileged, the have-nots and the haves. Catholics felt cut off not only because they lacked an effective political voice, but because they suffered marked disadvantages in employment and housing.

On Sunday, January 30, 1972, Catholics in the British-ruled Northern Ireland city of Londonderry set out on a civil rights march, when violence suddenly erupted in the streets. Shots rang out as British paratroopers, attempting to halt the demonstration, killed fourteen Catholic civilian marchers. Although it was later alleged that the paratroopers had been fired upon, no British soldiers were killed or injured. Bloody Sunday, as the Londonderry episode was known, came to be regarded as the symbol of

British oppression in Northern Ireland, and it sparked decades of terrorist activity.

The goal of the PIRA was to oust the British and to unite Northern Ireland with the Republic of Ireland. During the 1970s, the Provos used a variety of bombing devices to terrorize the British occupiers of Northern Ireland. The targets they chose were military and police barracks, administrative and government buildings, and electricity transformers. Cinemas, pubs, dance halls, and hotels where the British soldiers relaxed were also on the list, as were business firms, factories, and stores under British ownership.

Also in the 1970s, the PIRA became allied with the international terrorist network. Its leadership met in Lebanon with George Habash, the head of the Popular Front for the Liberation of Palestine (PFLP), at a so-called terrorist summit. Habash was among the most violent advocates of death in his campaign to evict the Jews from Israel and to place that territory in the hands of the Palestinians.

The Provos attended terrorist training camps in the Middle East, where they learned new and more sophisticated tactics. They also received money and arms from their new allies in exchange for providing safe houses (places of refuge from the law) for Arab terrorists in Ireland and England.

On August 27, 1979, the PIRA killed Lord Louis Mountbatten, the British World War II hero, by blowing up his boat as he fished in Donegal Bay, off the northwest coast of Ireland. On the same day, eighteen British soldiers stationed in Northern Ireland were killed by a remote-controlled bomb.

Emboldened by their success in the development of long-distance bomb-detonating mechanisms, the Provos accelerated their operations in England, where they undertook a series of bombings in London and other sites on British soil. In 1984, they attempted to kill Prime Minister Margaret Thatcher and her cabinet.

In advance of an annual government convention to be held at the Grand Hotel in the seaside resort of Brighton, PIRA terrorists, led by Patrick Magee, planted bombs at the conference site and at other locations where British citizens and foreign tourists might gather. The explosives would be detonated at selected hours by a timing device powered by a computer microchip.

At 2:54 A.M. on October 12, 1984, a 30-pound (14-kg) bomb planted in the bathroom paneling of Room 629 in the Grand Hotel went off with a terrific blast. It killed five persons and injured thirty-four. Margaret Thatcher, however, was unharmed. Magee was sentenced to a minimum of thirty-five years in a British prison for the 1984 assassination attempt.

The tragedy of Northern Ireland, however, is that the terrorist mindset strongly influences the children of both Protestants and Catholics from one generation to the next. Young people grow up exposed to terror and violence on the local level. A Protestant child sees his older brother killed in a bloody neighborhood confrontation with Catholic youths. A young Catholic child is made to walk between columns of jeering Protestants on her way to her grade-school classroom.

In spite of repeated cease-fires in the 1990s, so that talks about more autonomy for Northern Ireland might begin, peace between the rival factions—Catholics and Protestants, Catholics and British authorities—seemed out of reach. PIRA bombs continued to be exploded in London and, on the local level, violent street battles flared up all too frequently.

In early January 2002, several days of rioting broke out in a divided district of the city of Belfast. Police, trying to keep enraged Catholics and Protestants apart, were attacked by more than 350 young people from both sides, hurling gasoline bombs, acid bombs, stones, bricks, and bottles, many of them thrown from rooftops. Several police vehicles were set on fire, and seventeen cars parked on the grounds of a Catholic school had their windows smashed.

Police, ever careful to avoid a repeat of 1972's Bloody Sunday, used plastic bullets, and only sparingly, to try to subdue the crowd. As a result, several dozen officers were wounded. The question of whether the long-simmering violence arising from the Irish rebellion would ever come to an end in Northern Ireland remained unresolved.

The PIRA has not been alone in its use of terrorism to try to achieve the political goal of an independent homeland. Among the Basque people of Spain is another nationalist-separatist movement that employs violence.

The Basques have lived in the foothills of the Pyrenees Mountains, in northeast Spain and southwest France, since ancient Roman times at least. They have their own customs and traditions and a very unusual language. While ethnologists do not classify the Basques as a distinct race, linguists have searched in vain for a tongue related to the Basque language.

The movement for an independent homeland in north-central Spain took formal shape in 1959 with the founding of the Euskadi ta Askatasuna (ETA). The Basque words translate roughly into "Basque Homeland and Liberty." In 1975, after the death of the repressive Spanish dictator, Francisco Franco, terrorist activities escalated, with bombings, kidnappings, and assassinations. Although limited autonomy was granted to the Basques in 1979, the ETA has killed more than 800 people in Spain since the 1960s. It also operates to a lesser extent in France.

Targets have been Spanish government officials and military and security personnel, as well as journalists and university-level teachers and academicians, in both the Basque region and elsewhere in Spain. The ETA has also attempted to scare off tourists, particularly those vacationing on the Basque coasts. In one incident in the 1990s, twenty-four foreign tourists on a charter flight from Britain were injured by an explosive device concealed in a paper bag that had been planted in the women's bathroom at the local airport. In June 2002, British tourists were again targeted in a series of bombings at Spanish coastal resorts. Minor injuries occurred.

Basque moderates, individuals who oppose the violence of the ETA, have also been victims of the terror organization. Car dealerships, discotheques, and other enterprises run by the Basque business community have been bombed and, in some cases, the ETA has murdered their owners.

Although 60 percent of those killed by the ETA have been members of the Spanish security forces, ordinary Spanish citizens are also in danger, especially in such public gathering places as banks and railway stations. In 1995, a car bomb that was detonated in the center of Madrid, the Spanish capital, killed six bystanders and wounded fifteen. The ETA declares that it undertakes such actions to draw the attention of the international community and to demonstrate the powerlessness of the Spanish government.

As in the case of the youth of Ireland, young Basques are drawn to the separatist-nationalist ideals espoused by their elders. In April of 2000, a youth wing of the ETA

41

announced itself at a meeting in France, claiming to have 20,000 supporters. Calling itself *Haika*, Basque for "rising up," the new organization represented a merging of both Spanish and French pro-independence groups.

ETA was proud of the "new growth" its terrorism had spawned. But a police official called Haika a "greenhouse" for future killers. The official predicted that, as in the case of most young terrorists, Haika members were likely to start by throwing stones and bottles, and to escalate their attacks to car bombings and assassinations.

Yet another separatist group, one that has been drawing attention on the terrorist scene since 1983, is that of the Tamil people of Sri Lanka (formerly Ceylon), an island nation off the southeast coast of India.

The population of Sri Lanka is 74 percent Sinhalese, most of them Buddhists. The Tamils, who invaded from southern India in very early times, make up about 18 percent of the population, and are mainly Hindus. Strong rivalries have existed between the Sinhalese majority and the Tamil minority for centuries.

Foreign powers ruled the island until it achieved independence in 1948. In 1960, the Sinhalese majority decreed that Sinhalese was to be the official language of Sri Lanka, setting off demonstrations by the Tamils for the preservation of their own language in the northern and eastern provinces where they lived.

Although the language law was suspended in 1966, a campaign for a completely independent Tamil state in northeastern Sri Lanka began to gather strength. The name of the separatist movement, founded in 1976, was the Liberation Tigers of Tamil Eelam (LTTE). Seven years later, in 1983, civil war broke out between the LTTE and the Sri Lankan government.

The 1990s were a particularly violent time, during which the Tamils fought a guerrilla war with government forces and also carried out a number of terrorist acts. In 1991, a Tamil suicide bomber assassinated Rajiv Gandhi, India's former prime minister, during a campaign rally in which Gandhi was trying to make a comeback. The killing was in retaliation for India's having sent troops to Sri Lanka to try to suppress the Tamil rebellion.

On May Day in 1993, Sinhalese president Ranasinghe Premadasa—who had been democratically elected in 1988—was assassinated by a suicide bomber believed to be a Tamil rebel. In all, since 1983, 64,000 lives have been lost in the fighting for a Tamil homeland.

Cease-fires have been declared from time to time, based on promises of limited autonomy for all of Sri Lanka's provinces, including the Tamil northeast. A 1995 cease-fire ended after fourteen weeks, with Tamil terrorists blowing up two government gunboats. Another proposal for a cease-fire and for peace talks was drawn up in December 2001. Talks, which began in the early months of 2002, were still taking place in January 2003. Whether they would succeed in ending nineteen years of civil war and of terrorist operations by the LTTE was yet to be seen.

4
The
Palestinians

Far more intense than the terrorism of the Irish Provos or the Basque separatists—and infinitely more costly in terms of human life—has been the ongoing struggle of the Palestinian militants in the state of Israel.

The history of the territory formerly known as Palestine, and earlier as the biblical Holy Land, is one of both religious and national strife. As long ago as ancient Roman times, a Jewish terrorist sect known as the Zealots operated in Jerusalem. From C.E. [Common Era] 6 on, their goal was to throw off the yoke of Roman occupation.

The Zealots' weapon of choice was the *sica*, a dagger that they concealed in the folds of their robes. Lurking in the crowded marketplaces and the temple forecourts of the city, the Sicarii skillfully slit the throats of Roman officials and soldiers. They then disappeared into the mingling hordes. Jews who had dealings with the Roman official-dom, or were otherwise considered to be pro-Roman, were also among the targets of the Zealots. In C.E. 66 the Zealots led the Jews in a general uprising against the Romans that ended in defeat in C.E. 73.

Jewish terrorists once again appeared in Palestine during the time of the British mandate. Starting in 1922, Great Britain had, with the approval of the League of Nations, been administering the disputed territory. Since the late 1800s, Jews from Europe known as Zionists, who considered Palestine their ancient homeland, had been immigrating to that troubled area. Arab peoples also lived in Palestine, a poor and neglected wasteland.

As anticolonialist and national liberation movements arose in the aftermath of World War II, the drive to oust the occupying powers gained momentum. This was true in Palestine as well. Jewish pioneers living in that territory became vigorous in their pursuit of freedom from the British occupation. They formed militant groups known as the Haganah, the Stern Gang, and the Irgun Zvai Leumi.

The Haganah was a secret home guard organized for the purpose of protecting Jewish settlers against Arab belligerents. It developed a spy operation to intercept attacks on Jewish life and property, and it supplied its members with arms even though it was illegal to do so under the British mandate.

When Abraham Stern immigrated to Palestine from Poland in 1922, he became a charter member of the Haganah. Stern, who had experienced anti-Semitism in Eastern Europe and whose ancestors had for decades been the victims of pogroms—organized massacres of Jews—did not feel the Haganah was severe enough in its response to

Arab attacks on Jews. He then joined and later split from the Irgun to form an anti-Arab, anti-British commando group known as the Stern Gang, which also called itself the Freedom Fighters for Israel.

It has been said that one man's terrorist is another man's freedom fighter. The distinction, however, appears to depend on which side one is on. The bombings and assassinations carried out by the Stern Gang against Arab villages, as well as British police and British military fortifications, marked it as a terrorist group.

Abraham Stern was shot and killed by the British police in 1942, but the Stern Gang continued its efforts to remove the British from Palestine. On November 6, 1944, the Stern Gang assassinated Lord Moyne, the British minister for Middle East affairs, in Cairo. In 1947, the Stern Gang sent mail bombs to Ernest Bevin, the British foreign secretary in London, and to Anthony Eden, who had been his predecessor. Both escaped injury. But on September 17, 1948, soon after the creation of the state of Israel, the Stern Gang assassinated the Swedish diplomat Count Folke Bernadotte in Jerusalem. Bernadotte, who was the United Nations mediator for a partition of Israeli territory between Arabs and Jews, seemed to favor the Arabs.

The Irgun was another Jewish terrorist group operating in Palestine. It began to press for an independent Jewish state in the late 1930s, but suspended most of its anti-British activities until World War II began to draw to a close. Menachem Begin, who arrived in Palestine in 1942—and who would serve as prime minister of Israel from 1977 to 1983—became a commander of Irgun.

Irgun's efforts to force Britain to give up its mandate climaxed in the July 22, 1946, bombing of Jerusalem's King David Hotel. The hotel was targeted because it housed British administrative and military headquarters. The blast killed ninety-one people and injured forty-five, including many Jewish and Arab civilians who happened to be on the site or in the vicinity.

Between 1945 and 1947, at least 150 British soldiers stationed in Palestine met their deaths at the hands of Jewish militants. Finally, on May 14, 1948, the goal of independence was realized. Great Britain withdrew its mandate and its military forces from Palestine, which overnight became the State of Israel, a homeland for the numerous Jewish survivors of the Nazi death camps, as well as the displaced Jews of war-torn Europe and other parts of the world.

The achievement of Israeli independence poses the question of whether terrorism can ever succeed. While it is true that the actions of the Stern Gang and Irgun were destructive to British morale and British administrative efforts in Palestine, there were a number of other factors that accounted for the British withdrawal.

In addition to the sweeping postwar movement opposing colonialism in the Middle East—as well as in Asia and Africa—there were specific pressures on Great Britain. The nation was suffering the costs of World War II, financially and psychologically; pro-Zionist groups around the world were demanding a homeland for the tens of thousands of Jewish Holocaust survivors; and the United States was strongly in favor of the creation of a Jewish state.

Just before the British withdrawal in 1948, the United Nations had adopted a plan to divide Palestine into an Arab state and a Jewish state. The Jews of Palestine accepted the partition plan, but the Arabs rejected it. With this began the conflict that remains unresolved to this day. A fierce Palestinian nationalism was created, which, in due course, gave rise to a host of Palestinian terrorist organizations operating both within Israel and beyond its borders.

On May 15, 1948, one day after it had declared statehood, Israel was invaded by its Arab neighbors, including Egypt, Jordan (known as Transjordan until 1949), Lebanon, and Syria. Iraq and Saudi Arabia also took part in the attack to demonstrate their antagonism to the existence of a Jewish state in the Middle East, as did Palestinian guerrillas.

The 1948 war resulted in Israel's obtaining substantial additional land in the former Palestine, but it lost control of the Gaza Strip (in the west) to Egypt and the West Bank of the Jordan River (in the east) to Jordan. Approximately 750,000 Palestinian Arabs fled the fighting, either for fear of Israeli massacres or to avoid being caught in the crossfire, and became refugees in other Arab lands.

The plight of the displaced Palestinian Arabs led to the formation (in 1964 in Jordan), of the Palestine Liberation Organization (PLO). It began as a political body with the goal of creating a national homeland for Palestinians on Israeli soil. But militant elements that existed within the PLO soon dominated the organization. They included such terrorist factions as al-Fatah, started by Yasir Arafat and others in the mid-1950s, and the Popular Front for the Liberation of Palestine (PFLP), founded in the 1960s by George Habash.

On June 5, 1967, Israel launched the Six-Day War against its Arab neighbors, recapturing the Gaza Strip from Egypt and the West Bank from Jordan, as well as gaining other territory. As a result, Palestinian militants became more active. In 1968, al-Fatah joined the PLO and, the following year, Yasir Arafat was elected as its chairman. The PLO backed terrorist raids across the border into Israel, first from Jordan and later from Lebanon. The attacks targeted Israeli schools and marketplaces, bus stations and airports—any place where crowds of Israelis were likely to gather.

Like most terrorist groups, however, the Palestinian nationalists sought recognition beyond the borders of the targeted region. They saw a need to establish themselves on the global scene so that their cause would attract as large an audience as possible. George Habash of the PFLP felt strongly about using the world press and television for this purpose.

By 1968, following the launching of the first television (TV) satellites by the United States during the 1960s, TV coverage had expanded, leading to a revolution in mass communications. On August 17, 1969, Habash's PFLP set off an incendiary bomb in Marks and Spencer, a Jewish-owned London department store. In an interview with Italian journalist Oriana Fallaci that appeared in the June 22, 1970, issue of *Life* magazine, Habash declared, "When we set fire to a store in London, those few flames are worth the burning down of two kibbutzim [Israeli communal farm settlements] because we force people to ask what is going on . . ."

A bid for even greater terrorist notoriety took place in September 1972, when another Palestinian splinter group, known as Black September, launched a deadly attack on Israeli athletes taking part in the Olympic games in Munich, Germany.

Black September took its name to protest the policies of Jordan's King Hussein, who expelled a group of Palestinian terrorists from Jordan in September 1970. The operation was paid for in large part by Libyan leader

Can Terrorism Ever Succeed?

In his book *The Lessons of Terror: A History of Warfare Against Civilians: Why It Has Always Failed and Why It Will Fail Again*, Caleb Carr discusses the activities of the Stern Gang and the Irgun as factors in bringing about the departure of the British and the creation of the State of Israel.

Carr does not feel, however, that there were any positive values in the bitter campaign against the British. He states, in fact, that "the strain of vicious terrorism that the Irgun had bred into the Israeli character would never be removed. Worst of all, it would inspire vengeful imitation among the Palestinian Arabs."

He wrote:

When the Palestinians formed those groups whose names were in time to become so familiar . . . they took as their organizational and operational models the Irgun. . . . Had they not witnessed over many years the murderous efficiency of the Irgun, the Palestinians might have been tempted to choose a different path; but anger, desperation, and impatience took them down the same road, and inevitably, the results of their decision were also similar.

In other words, Carr tells us that terrorism cannot succeed in and of itself, but only in breeding more terrorism.

Colonel Muammar Qaddafi, who came on the scene at about that time as an advocate of international Islamic terrorism. His support was based on the principle that Muslims from all parts of the Middle East should back the Palestinian cause.

Shortly before dawn on September 5, 1972, eight well-trained terrorist commandos climbed the fence surrounding the Olympic compound and broke into Building 31, where the Israeli athletes were housed. The terrorists carried athletic-equipment bags that actually contained hand grenades and machine guns.

They immediately murdered two of the eleven Israelis and stated their intention of killing one more every two hours unless 236 terrorists (234 Arabs and 2 German terrorists) were released from Israeli jails. They also demanded an airplane to fly them and their captives to Egypt.

German authorities agreed to fly the eight Black September terrorists and their nine Israeli hostages by helicopter to a German airbase, where an aircraft would be waiting. Secretly, however, the Germans hoped to free the Israelis before the terrorists could board the plane.

German sharpshooters waiting at the airbase attempted to separate the hostages from their captives, but the operation was difficult and badly bungled. In the melee that followed, the terrorists shot the nine remaining Israelis. Also, the Germans killed five of the eight terrorists, while the remaining three were taken prisoner.

The horror of the slayings was seen on television around the world by an estimated 500 million viewers. While most of the global viewers strongly condemned the attack, the terrorists believed that the exposure had boosted the cause of Palestinian nationalism, spread terrorist ideas and techniques, and most certainly recruited additional supporters.

The terrorist philosophy was based on an ancient Chinese proverb: "Kill one; frighten 10,000." While the deaths of eleven Israelis could not possibly impair Israel's military strength, it was bound to deepen the fears of all Israelis and their supporters worldwide.

The Munich tragedy concluded in late October of that year with the three surviving terrorists being flown to Libya, where they were freed in exchange for the return of a hijacked German airplane, presumably through negotiations between German and Libyan authorities.

Violence caused by Palestinian nationalism and Israeli reprisal continued to manifest itself throughout the 1970s. In a courageous move to initiate an international peace between Arabs and Jews, Egypt's president Anwar el-Sadat approached the Israeli prime minister Menachem Begin in November 1977, with the proposal that Egypt and Israel open a dialogue. Begin welcomed the suggestion and, in a historic goodwill gesture, Sadat flew to Jerusalem.

The following year the talks continued in the United States under the auspices of President Jimmy Carter and, on March 26, 1979, a peace agreement between Egypt and Israel was signed at Camp David, Maryland. Both leaders received the Nobel Peace Prize for their act of conciliation. But the militant Islamic regimes of the Middle East, as well as extremist elements in Sadat's Egypt, were strongly opposed to Sadat's bid for peace. They saw him as betraying their cause, which was the denial of Israel's right to exist.

On October 6, 1981, Anwar El-Sadat sat with members of his government on a reviewing stand in Cairo, watching a military procession of Egyptian troops and a simultaneous

Egyptian air force flyover. As Sadat gazed at the Mirage jets overhead, one of the passing army vehicles came to a halt directly in front of the reviewing stand. Five men in army uniforms leaped from the truck. With cries of "Kill the traitor!" they tossed hand grenades into the reviewing stand and sprayed it with gunfire.

Sadat, who had been struck with four carefully aimed bullets, died in the hospital two hours later. Eleven other members of Sadat's party were murdered as well, and a number of military guards were killed. Dozens of people were wounded.

Sadat's assassins were members of the terrorist sect Takfir Wal-Hajira, "Repentance of the Holy Flight," sponsored by Muammar Qaddafi of Libya. The main

UNDER THE AUSPICES OF PRESIDENT JIMMY CARTER, PRESIDENT ANWAR EL-SADAT OF EGYPT AND PRIME MINISTER MENACHEM BEGIN OF ISRAEL MET, ON SEPTEMBER 18, 1978, IN WASHINGTON, D.C., FOR PEACE TALKS.

"The Media Must Report Terrorism"

As it became increasingly evident in the 1970s and the 1980s that terrorists could and would use media coverage to their advantage, government officials and media executives debated the question of whether acts of terrorism should be reported.

British Prime Minister Margaret Thatcher was of the opinion that "We must try to find ways to starve the terrorist and the hijacker of the oxygen of publicity on which they depend."

Katharine Graham, publisher of *The Washington Post*, disagreed. While Graham admitted that it was true that terrorism required an audience in order to survive, she asserted the need for a free flow of information. Her reasons included the following: "Terrorist acts are impossible to ignore. If the media did not report them, rumor would abound."

Further, Graham stated, "Our citizens have a right to know what the government is doing to resolve crises and curb terrorist attacks. Some of the proposed solutions raise disturbing questions about when the United States should use military force."

In short, Graham said, "I believe the harm of restricting coverage surpasses the evils of broadcasting."

participants were Egyptians whose fellow militants had been jailed by Sadat in an effort to repress Islamic fanaticism in Egypt. They included both military officers and civilians. The military officers who had taken part in the conspiracy were executed by firing squad, and the civilians who had posed as soldiers were hanged. Seventeen others were imprisoned. But the threat of reprisal for Egypt's peace efforts continued to simmer. In a 1986 interview with the German magazine *Der Spiegel* the arch-Palestinian terrorist Abu Nidal declared that Sadat's peace accord "has gone under with him. It is only a question of time before Sadat's follower, Hosni Mubarak [successor to Sadat as president of Egypt], will also pay dearly for his betrayal of Arab history . . ."

The following year, 1987, saw the outbreak of a new type of warfare in Israel called an *intifada*. The word in Arabic refers to shaking off bugs or other evils but is popularly translated as an "uprising." It began in the onetime Gaza Strip and the West Bank, both of which were occupied at the time by Israel. In ongoing pursuit of a Palestinian state, youths began a widespread campaign of civil disobedience, which on occasion turned violent. Israeli authorities responded with an increased police and military presence in the troubled areas, and the violence escalated.

The intifada had the backing of Hamas and Islamic Jihad, two Palestinian Muslim fundamentalist groups that favored an armed struggle rather than a political solution. In time, the intifada, which had begun as a series of street demonstrations, became a terrorist operation.

The political arm of the PLO, meanwhile, appeared to be heading in the direction of some sort of compromise with Israel. In a surprise peace initiative—not unlike that of Anwar el-Sadat in 1977—PLO leader Yasir Arafat and Israeli prime minister Yitzhak Rabin signed an agreement on September 13, 1993, calling for limited Palestinian self-rule in the Gaza Strip and part of the West Bank. The new entity would be known as the Palestinian Authority, and the peace accord (which had been negotiated in Oslo, Norway), was signed in Washington, D.C., on the White House lawn. The following year, 1994, both Arafat and Rabin received Nobel Peace Prizes.

In spite of repeated acts of disruption by Hamas and other militant Palestinian groups, a second agreement was signed on September 28, 1995, extending Palestinian self-rule to more of the West Bank, including its refugee camps. Weeks later, on November 4, 1995, Israeli prime minister Yitzhak Rabin was assassinated at a public gathering. His murderer was an Israeli extremist, a law student named Yigal Amir, who opposed the peace process, largely because he saw Palestinian self-rule as threatening to the communities of Jewish settlers that existed in the West Bank. Once again, as in the case of President Anwar el-Sadat of Egypt, a national leader who took the risk of seeking a peaceful solution to the Palestinian-Israeli conflict had been eliminated by the forces of right-wing extremism.

A third major bid for peace began in July 1999, when yet another Israeli prime minister, Ehud Barak, met with chairman of the PLO, Yasir Arafat. At the peace talks, which took place at Camp David during the administration of President Bill Clinton, Barak offered Arafat a self-governed Palestinian state. It would include the entire Gaza Strip, nearly all of the West Bank, and authority over part of Jerusalem—a total of 97 percent of the land in question. He also promised a rollback of Jewish settlements in the West Bank and elsewhere on Palestinian lands.

To the despair of all who hoped for an end to the half-century of war and terrorism in Israel, Yasir Arafat refused the Israeli offer (and formal talks were suspended on July 25, 2000). He did so, in part, because it did not include a "right of return" to Israel by all those Palestinians who had become refugees in other Arab nations as a result of the 1948 war.

In fifty-two years, the number of refugees had grown from hundreds of thousands to four million. The relatively tiny State of Israel could not possibly absorb such a huge number of "returnees." Yet, despite an offer made as late as January 2001 to accept a symbolic number of returnees and make reparations payments to the rest, Chairman Arafat's refusal of the Israeli offer was final, leading many Western observers to wonder if peace through the creation of a self-governed Palestinian state was really Arafat's goal. Arab and Muslim observers, on the other hand, agreed with Arafat in assessing the peace proposal as limited and inadequate.

In September 2000, rising tensions among both Israelis and Palestinians erupted in what became known as the second intifada. It took the form of a cycle of suicide bombings and other attacks on Israeli civilians by Palestinian terrorists, and of Israeli retaliations in the form of military incursions into the Palestinian territories that sheltered the terrorists.

The intifada was seen as having been triggered by Palestinian anger at the failure of the Camp David peace efforts. It was also seen as having been related to the controversial visit by Ariel Sharon, on September 28, 2000, to the Temple Mount near the al-Aqsa Mosque in Jerusalem, the holiest Muslim site in Israel.

Sharon, who was elected prime minister of Israel in

February 2001, was a retired army general. He had been a commander in every major conflict with the Arabs since 1948, and had been opposed to the peace negotiations undertaken by his predecessor, Ehud Barak. Sharon's presence at the Muslim site in September 2000 appeared to send a signal of defiance to Arafat, Sharon's longtime enemy, and to the more violent elements in the Palestinian camp.

The intifada that began within days of Sharon's appearance on the Temple Mount did not begin with unarmed Palestinian youths throwing rocks, as in 1987. Since 1993, young men who had been languishing in Israel's refugee camps and occupied territories had been presenting themselves to terrorist sponsors as willing suicide bombers. They were ready to blow themselves up on buses, in the streets, and in stores and cafes where Israelis gathered, taking with them as many victims as possible.

The final months of the year 2000 saw a marked increase in terrorist activity in Israeli settlements and cities. Like their predecessors, the new volunteers for martyrdom were imbued with the Islamic fundamentalist belief that dying for Palestinian statehood would open the gates of Paradise to them.

For the Palestinian suicide bomber, the preparation for death began with pledging oneself to the holy struggle. It was said that the moment of death, "if done for Allah's sake, [hurt] less than a gnat's bite." Hamas and Islamic Jihad were the chief recruiters of terrorist volunteers. Usually they were men between the ages of eighteen and thirty-five. In January 2002, women began to join the ranks of the Palestinian suicide bombers. Many of them were recruited by the al-Aqsa Martyrs Brigade—a secular rather than religious group (such as Hamas and Islamic Jihad). The al-Aqsa Brigade was closely related to al-Fatah, a faction of the PLO believed to be under the direct sponsorship of Chairman Arafat.

Unlike the jobless, stone-throwing youths of the 1980s, many of the suicide bombers of the early 2000s were middle-class, university-educated, and even held good jobs. They had also studied the Koran, learned passages by heart, and saw themselves as martyrs rather than suicides. Young women who gave their lives asserted that the Koran did not deny females permission to join the holy war. Often, the prospective suicide prepared a written statement, an audiotape, or a videotape just before his or her mission. These declarations of intent to die for the holy cause were then circulated to inspire others to follow their example. It was reported that the sponsoring terror groups made payments as high as tens of thousands of dollars to the families of the martyrs. Some families held celebrations in honor of the sacrifice of a son or daughter. But others were numbed with grief.

The year 2002 saw a hard-line response by the government of Ariel Sharon to the escalating number of Palestinian terror attacks. Between 1993 and September 2000, there had been 61 attempted and successful suicide bombings. Between September 2000 and mid-June 2002, there had been 116, resulting in an unprecedented number of Israeli civilian deaths.

Twenty-nine people were killed in a single episode on March 27, 2002—the night of the first seder [ceremonial dinner] of the Jewish Passover—when a suicide bomber entered the banquet hall of the Park Hotel in the Israeli seaside resort of Netanya. Restaurants and supermarkets, social clubs and cafes, buses and police checkpoints had been the sites of ongoing killings of Israeli civilians by Palestinian terrorists for months.

In April 2002, in an effort to stem the Palestinian terror rampage, Israel made the first of several heavily armored military incursions into Palestinian West Bank cities, including the Ramallah compound of Yasir Arafat, where the PLO chairman was virtually held prisoner for a time.

The Israeli incursions inevitably cost the lives of innocent Palestinians, and saw the destruction of Palestinian homes and infrastructure. The incursions also led to the arrest of a number of Palestinian terrorists and to temporary respites from the almost daily attacks of the suicide bombers. Yasir Arafat, who had appeared to be unwilling or unable to control Palestinian terrorism, spoke out at last in a denunciation of the killing of Israeli civilians. But as soon as the Israeli military withdrew from the Palestinian cities, the cycle of violence returned and again incursions were made into the terrorists' strongholds.

The answers in the Palestinian-Israeli conflict were hard to find. Could military strikes in which innocent Palestinians died be justified? Could suicide bombings that killed more and more Israelis be allowed to continue? Most importantly, how could both sides be persuaded to try to overcome the obstacles on the shattered road to peace?

There were a number of matters that had not been resolved during previous peace talks. They included full agreement on the permanent borders of a Palestinian state within Israel; a decision with regard to the dismantling of Jewish settlements in the Palestinian lands; an answer to the question of Palestinian authority over Muslim sites in Jerusalem; and a realistic handling of the refugee return problem.

If the current leaders of the Palestinian and Israeli factions were too immersed in hatred and bitterness resulting from their long struggle, would new ones come along, capable of accomplishing a true and lasting peace? Would Palestinians and Israelis eventually bring such leaders to the forefront?

In early 2001, following the confirmed failure of the

peace efforts of the summer of 2000, Saeb Erekat, Arafat's chief negotiator, stated, "My heart aches because we were so close. At the end of the day . . . I know Palestinians and Israelis can make peace. If it's not next year, if it's not in ten years, peace will come . . . and the difference between this moment and the moment of reaching an agreement will be how many names will be added to the lists of death and agony."

5
The New Left

In the Middle East, Africa, and Asia, the years following the conclusion of World War II gave rise to demands for national liberation. In Europe and the United States, the postwar era saw a groundswell of other kinds of social and political demands. Young people, largely middle-class and university-educated, rose up against the capitalist, highly industrialized, and militaristic societies of the western powers.

The United States was a target, both at home and abroad, because of the prolonged Vietnam War in which it had become engaged in the 1960s. The young rebels were also critical of the materialism and the new affluence of the postwar societies in which they lived. In other words, they were opposed to the preoccupation with acquiring goods and money. They sought to develop a counterculture, a less materialistic lifestyle—one that often included drug use and sexual freedoms.

Politically, the rebels tended to identify with the most revolutionary leftist parties in their home countries. Yet, they did not generally become members of the mainstream communist parties. Their goal appeared to be to break new ground. For this reason, they came to be known as the New Left.

Many of the New Left groups limited their activities to meetings and to peaceful demonstrations. But others became terror groups. One of the most notorious was the Baader-Meinhof Gang in Germany, which was formed in 1967 as an outgrowth of the student rebellions of the early 1960s.

The group was named for its ruthless female leader, Ulrike Meinhof, who had been born in 1934 to educated, well-to-do parents, and for Andreas Baader, a sometime playboy and a heavy user of drugs, who was born in 1943. As the driving force in the group, Meinhof declared that its object was "to hit the Establishment in the face, to mobilize the masses, and to maintain international solidarity."

Yet, in spite of all its fiery and idealistic talk, the Baader-Meinhof Gang—which in 1970 began to call itself the Red Army Faction (RAF)—showed little concern for the welfare of working people. Its political aims, in fact, were vague enough to be labeled as nihilism, or the denial of any existing truths with regard to government or other institutions. In other words, the RAF wanted to destroy the social and political system of Germany, but it had no concrete plan for replacing the existing system.

To strengthen its campaign to take power from what Ulrike Meinhof labeled Europe's "ruling class," the RAF made contact with the Popular Front for the Liberation of

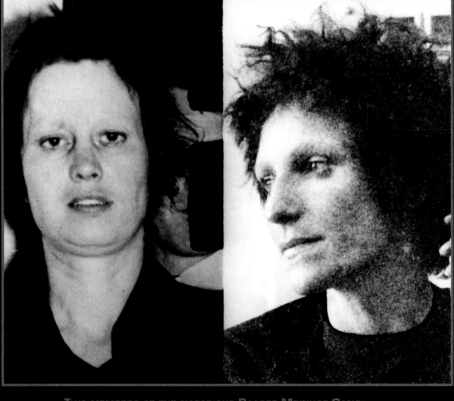

TWO MEMBERS OF THE NOTORIOUS BAADER-MEINHOF GANG:
ULRIKE MEINHOF (LEFT), AND GUDRUN ENSSLIN.

Palestine (PFLP), and arranged to receive training in terrorist tactics in the Middle East. In 1970, Meinhof and a contingent of male and female gang members spent a number of months in camps in Lebanon and Jordan. There the gang members learned the various aspects of urban guerrilla warfare, including commando raids, marksmanship, making bombs, kidnapping, and bank robbery. Kidnappings and bank robberies would help to finance the group's other operations.

Soon, more than 150 well-trained RAF members were distributed around West Germany, in underground cells of five persons each, and were launching brazen attacks on individuals and institutions that they saw as economic exploiters or political oppressors. Ruthlessly, the RAF raided police arsenals to obtain firearms and ammunition, stole getaway cars, and murdered in cold blood any officials or civilians who crossed their path during their terror operations.

The RAF did not limit its attacks to German targets. It considered the United States an archenemy because of its economic and political influence on Germany and other Western European nations. On May 11 and again on May 24, 1972, the RAF bombed U. S. Army headquarters in Germany, the first in Frankfurt and the second in Heidelberg. Three American military officers died as a result of the attacks, more than a dozen other service personnel were seriously wounded, and there was extensive property damage. The RAF stated that the attack was in retaliation for America's involvement in the Vietnam War.

It took until 1975 for the German government to charge Ulrike Meinhof, and until 1976 to put her on trial, along with Andreas Baader and a second fanatical female leader, Gudrun Ensslin. On May 9, 1976, Meinhof, who was condemned to a long prison term, was found hanged in her jail cell with a rope made from a towel torn into strips. Four thousand supporters, many of them masked, were said to have attended her funeral in West Berlin on May 16, 1976.

Baader and Ensslin languished in jail until 1977, when Baader committed suicide with a smuggled gun and Ensslin hanged herself, using the same technique as Meinhof. Even without its original leadership, the RAF continued to kidnap and either hold for ransom or murder business and political leaders. Its final terrorist act during its major period of activity was the kidnapping of the German industrialist Hanns-Martin Schleyer.

One of the demands of the kidnappers, following the suicides of Baader and Ensslin, was the release of eleven RAF members who were still in jail. The German government refused to bow to the terrorists. On October 19, 1977, the RAF murdered Schleyer. His body was found stuffed in the trunk of a car in Mulhouse, France, just over the German border.

The question of whether the Baader-Meinhof Gang/RAF dissolved permanently during the 1980s, or even after it declared a 1998 cease-fire, must remain uncertain. Prior to the September 11, 2001 Al Qaeda attack on the United States, it was generally believed that the New Left had long ago abandoned its activities. But on March 19, 2002, an Italian terror group, similar in origin and nature to the RAF, reared up in Italy. It had been encouraged to strike, the Italian group stated, by the "destabilizing effects" of the Islamic terrorist attacks on the United States.

The Italian Red Brigades, or Brigate Rosse (BR), was founded in 1969 by a group of leftist revolutionaries led by Renato Curcio. The stated aim of the BR was to produce "an armed proletariat vanguard to do battle against the imperialist state of the multinationals." In other words, the BR declared itself a defender of the working class. It also sought to separate Italy from its alliance with the United States and other western capitalist nations.

Like the RAF in Germany, the BR had grown out of the student rebellions of the 1960s and, for security purposes, it operated in cells of no more than five members. The cells were arranged in the pattern of a pyramid, and only one member of each cell had contact with the next higher cell. Also like the RAF, the BR refused to align itself with the established communist party. It felt that only the BR was the true standard-bearer of Marxist-Leninist ideology.

By the 1970s, Italy's New Left terror organization was kidnapping and assassinating industrialists and members of the Italian government who they termed "enemies of the people." They attacked Italian industry directly by blowing up the trucks of the tire manufacturer Pirelli. As the crimes of the BR mounted and its members were jailed, the cycle of violence escalated. On April 18, 1974, the BR kidnapped a government prosecutor, Mario Sossi, threatening to murder him unless the Italian government agreed to the release of eight jailed BR members. Sossi was released, but when the government stalled in its promise, the BR hunted down Sossi and killed him. This led to the jailing of Curcio and over a dozen more BR members.

The most notorious operation of the BR was the kidnapping and murder of Aldo Moro, who had served five times as prime minister of Italy, was a popular figure on the world scene, and was sympathetic to the problems of the working class. He worked with the socialist and communist parties in his government, supporting many of their causes, but he disdained the terrorist BR.

Moro was kidnapped on March 16, 1978, and was held at an unknown location for two months, during which time the BR sent cruelly confusing messages to his family and the press. Some reports promised his imminent release; others stated flatly that he was dead. On May 9, 1978, as a result of a tip to the police, Moro's body was found in the trunk of a car parked in Rome. His hands and feet were bound with chains and he had been shot eleven times.

Massive arrests of BR members followed the Moro slaying. Perhaps to strengthen its weakened structure, the BR now sought an alliance with the Palestine Liberation Organization (PLO). Unlike the RAF in Germany, the Italian terror group did not send members to training camps in the Middle East. It did, however, arrange to receive arms shipments for its own use from the PLO. In exchange, the BR provided secret storage depots in Italy where the PLO could hide its stockpiles of weapons.

Like most of the New Left groups of the 1960s and 1970s, the original BR appeared to have ceased its activities by the 1980s. Yet, on March 19, 2002, there was an event that sent shock waves through Italy. Marco Biagi, a government consultant who had been advocating anti-union labor changes designed to make Italy more competitive in the world marketplace, was gunned down as he was returning in the evening to his home in Bologna after work. Scrawled on the wall of the building was the five-pointed star of the Red Brigades.

One day after the murder, the existence of a second generation of Red Brigades was confirmed. The terror group that took responsibility for the murder now called itself the "Red Brigades for the Building of the Fighting Communist Party." Moreover, it was revealed that the new BR had also murdered an Italian labor minister, Massimo

D'Antona, on May 20, 1999. The same gun had been used in both the Biagi and the D'Antona killings.

While the reappearance of the New Left in Italy had resulted in relatively few terrorist incidents thus far, other developed nations wondered if their presumably defunct New Left groups might spring to life again. In addition to Germany's Baader-Meinhof Gang, France had had its New Left terrorist group, known as L'Action Directe, and Japan had been held hostage in the 1970s by leftist militants calling themselves the Japanese Red Army.

In Greece, an underground group called November 17 has been active for about thirty years. It took its name from the date of a 1973 student riot at Athens Polytechnic Institute. Although it had claimed responsibility for twenty-three killings since its inception, Greek authorities had never apprehended a single suspect. Among the victims of November 17 had been the station chief of America's Central Intelligence Agency (CIA) in 1975. In May 1997, it assassinated a Greek-British shipping magnate and, in June 2000, a British military adviser stationed in Athens. There were long-held suspicions that November 17 had high-level connections within the government of Greece, but the identity of the group members remained mysterious.

On June 29, 2002, however, there was an initial breakthrough into the mystery of the terror group. A time bomb being transported to the Greek port city of Piraeus exploded, wounding a member of November 17. After taking the suspect into custody, the police were able to track the group's hideout in Athens, where they discovered a large weapons cache. On July 17, 2002, the first of the small group of leaders of the "phantom organization" was rooted out. The victory was a timely one for the nation, for the continuing presence of November 17 was seen as a serious threat to the success of the 2004 Summer Olympics, scheduled to take place in Athens.

In the United States, a New Left organization that had been active in the 1970s came back into the news some thirty years after its first appearance on the terrorist scene. The Symbionese Liberation Army (SLA) was one of several violent action groups, such as the Weathermen and the Black Panthers, that sprang from the student revolutionary movements of the 1960s and that included black-liberation militants as well.

The SLA was formed in 1973 in Oakland, California. Its leader was Donald DeFreeze, a black prison escapee, but many of its members were white, college-educated young people from middle-class families. The credo of the SLA was "Death to the fascist insect that preys upon the life of the people." It adopted as its symbol a seven-headed cobra.

DeFreeze preferred to be known as Field Marshall Cinque. DeFreeze, who had a long criminal record, de-clared war on the moneyed economy of the nation for the benefit of the underprivileged. On February 4, 1974, the SLA made headlines with its kidnapping of Patricia Campbell Hearst, the granddaughter of the publishing magnate William Randolph Hearst, and heir to the Hearst fortune. A ransom demand of millions of dollars for food for the poor was paid. But the food distribution turned into a profiteering operation for groups allied to the SLA, and Patricia Hearst was not returned to her family.

Some questions about the kidnapping are unanswered to this day. Nineteen-year-old Patty Hearst was abducted from the Berkeley, California, apartment that she shared with her fiancé, Steven Weed. Although Weed was badly

PATTY HEARST, THE AMERICAN HEIRESS KIDNAPPED BY THE SYMBIONESE LIBERATION ARMY IN 1974, WAS FILMED BY A SURVEILLANCE CAMERA IN 1975 AS SHE PARTICIPATED IN A BANK ROBBERY.

beaten by the SLA kidnappers, Hearst did not appear to have put up much of a struggle. There were rumors that she had had some previous contact with the SLA.

According to Hearst, however, she was brainwashed and became a criminal member of the SLA only after weeks of harsh treatment. She was blindfolded, kept in a closet, abused by gang members, and then forced to participate in a bank robbery in San Francisco on April 15, 1974. During the robbery, she was caught on a video camera holding a gun. Two bystanders had been wounded in the robbery and the SLA had stolen more than $10,000.

The newly revolutionized Patty Hearst now called herself Tania, after the girlfriend of the South American revolutionist, Che Guevara. Although DeFreeze and five other heavily armed members of the SLA were killed by police in a massive shootout at a house where they were hiding out in Los Angeles on May 17, 1974, Hearst continued to be active in the SLA.

A year later, on April 21, 1975, she drove one of the getaway cars in a bank robbery near Sacramento that resulted in the death of a forty-two-year-old woman, a mother of four, who was making a deposit of a church collection. Five months later, Hearst was captured by the Federal Bureau of Investigation (FBI) and charged with having committed armed robbery in the San Francisco bank holdup. She was subsequently sentenced to seven years in prison, but was released after twenty-two months, when President Jimmy Carter commuted her sentence. In January 2001, on his final day in office, President Bill Clinton granted Hearst a pardon, thus exempting her from further prosecution.

Other SLA members of the 1970s did not fare as well as Patricia Hearst, who married after her release

"Enter Patty Hearst, and Some Other Ghosts from the '60s"

As Sara Jane Olson, formerly Kathleen Soliah, and other onetime members of the SLA faced trial for bank robberies and murders committed during the 1970s, one could not help reviewing the apparently preferential treatment that had been granted to Patty Hearst by Presidents Jimmy Carter and Bill Clinton.

Brent Staples wrote in an editorial in *The New York Times* on February 1, 2002, "When the new trial begins, people visiting the Hearst case for the first time, or after a long season of forgetting, may feel that the only difference between Patricia Hearst Shaw, witness for the prosecution, and those at the defendants' table is that she had more money and influence."

In Patty Hearst's own "trial for bank robbery, her family spent a great deal of money trying to counter the impression that she was no different from the other Symbionese soldiers" and she might indeed have had to serve her seven years in prison if her family had not been able to prevail on President Carter to commute her sentence. Does this mean that there are separate standards of punishment for rich terrorists, with money and connections, as opposed to all the rest? If so, and especially in view of September 11, the public would be justified in reacting with indignation to lesser punishments for the privileged.

and renounced her former affiliation with the so-called liberation army that had engaged in serious criminal activity.

In June 1999, another former female member of the SLA came to the attention of the authorities and the media. She was a St. Paul, Minnesota, housewife known as Sara Jane Olson. Her true identity, however, was that of a onetime radical named Kathleen Soliah, who was wanted for having planted bombs under Los Angeles police cars in 1975. Soliah's attempt to blow up members of the Los Angeles police had been in retaliation for the 1974 shootout in which SLA leader Donald DeFreeze was killed.

In October 2001, Mrs. Olson pleaded guilty to the charge, which carried a penalty of twenty years to life in prison. Later she attempted to withdraw her guilty plea. By that time, however, the terrorist attack of September 11, 2001, on the United States had taken place, heightening fears of homegrown as well as international terror activity and demanding punishment for past terrorist crimes that had taken place at home.

As a result, Mrs. Olson plus four other former members of the SLA who had been involved in the April 21, 1975, bank robbery near Sacramento found themselves charged, in January 2002, with the death of Myrna Opsahl. Mrs. Opsahl was the forty-two-year-old woman who had been making a bank deposit at the time of the robbery.

Olson and three of the other four suspects (the fourth was still at large) were arrested in January 2002 and faced a trial at which Patty Hearst, now Patricia Hearst Shaw, was scheduled to appear as a witness. Of the many New Left terrorist groups that grew out of the 1960s, the SLA had the least developed political agenda and the shortest life. Yet in its two years of violent activity, it managed to grab the headlines and to turn up— nearly thirty years later—a group of aging terrorists that an aroused American public felt should be brought to justice.

6

In the Skies, on the Sea

What do terrorists want? The reasons behind their operations, both past and present, have fallen into various categories. The violence of the New Left terrorists grew out of political ideologies that advocated the redistribution of wealth and declared war on the economies of the developed nations of the world.

Other groups have chosen terror as a means of acquiring independence from a ruling power, or nationhood. Examples of such nationalist-separatist militants include the IRA in Ireland, the ETA in Spain, and the PLO in Israel.

Most recently, terrorism based on religious dogma has come to the fore, finding extreme expression in the Al

Qaeda attack on New York City and Washington, D.C., in September 2001.

Whatever the driving force behind the terrorist's lawless, premeditated act of violence against civilians or other noncombatants, the terrorist chooses the target and the site of the attack. Some terrorists have chosen individual victims, such as government officials, business leaders, or other high-profile figures, for kidnapping or assassination. Other groups have made it their goal to annihilate, or at least terrorize, as many individuals as possible in a single operation. With the conclusion of World War II and the development of commercial air travel on a major scale, terrorists found a new site for their operations—the passenger airplane.

The first rash of postwar airplane hijackings—soon to be known as skyjackings—included acts of air piracy that took place in the United States in the early 1960s and were the work of individuals rather than members of organized terrorist groups. On August 3, 1961, a thirty-eight-year-old unemployed car salesman named Leon Bearden boarded a Continental B-707 jet in Phoenix, Arizona. With Bearden, who had a criminal record for having committed robbery and forgery, was his sixteen-year-old son, Cody.

After the flight became airborne, Bearden and his son entered the cockpit. Bearden pointed a .38 caliber pistol at the pilot, Captain Byron D. Rickards, and ordered him to fly the plane to the communist nation of Cuba, where Bearden presumably felt he would be beyond reach of the law.

Captain Rickards, who had experienced a similar incident while piloting a plane in South America, gained time and advantage by explaining that he would have to make a refueling stop in El Paso, Texas. When the plane landed, FBI and police officials, notified by Rickards,

took Bearden into custody. He was subsequently convicted and sent to prison for life.

Other such attempted hijackings took place throughout the 1960s and were, for the most part, unsuccessful.
The would-be hijackers were mainly unstable individuals,
misfits and malcontents who for one reason or another
envisioned a better future in a nation that was on a hostile
footing with the United States. However, Fidel Castro, the
Cuban leader, refused most of the fugitives and, in 1969,
he made an agreement with the United States to return
them to their own country for trial.

Individuals living under Eastern European communist
regimes, trying to escape to the West, made up most of the
other would-be hijackers of the 1960s. It is estimated that
during the twenty-year period between 1949 and 1969,
airplane hijackings averaged five per year.

Skyjackings carried out by organized terror groups
became widespread in the 1970s, when Palestinian militants started a series of attacks on passenger aircraft,
choosing mainly international flights.

On the morning of June 27, 1976, an Air France Air-
bus, Flight 139, took off from Tel Aviv, Israel, bound for
Paris, with a scheduled stop en route in Athens, Greece. In
Athens, 38 passengers deplaned, and 58 new passengers
got on, for a total of 246 on board.

A little past noon, as flight attendants were preparing
lunch and the aircraft was climbing to its cruising altitude
of 31,000 feet (9,449 m), a young, blond man rose from
his seat and headed toward the cockpit door, which was
unlocked. Bursting into the pilots' quarters, he demanded
at gunpoint that Captain Michel Bacos fly the plane to
Libya for refueling.

In the first-class cabin, a twenty-five-year-old woman
of similarly fair appearance, and also armed, was holding

the passengers at bay, while two young Arab men with guns had subdued the passengers in the tourist compartment. All four of the hijackers had boarded the flight at Athens, having arrived there early that morning on a Singapore Airlines flight from Bahrain and Kuwait, two Persian Gulf Arab nations.

At Benghazi airport in Libya, the Arabs met with a representative of the group that had masterminded the operation, the Popular Front for the Liberation of Palestine (PFLP). The other two hijackers were Germans, traveling under false passports. They were members of the Baader-Meinhof Gang, or Red Army Faction (RAF), who had allied themselves with the Palestinian terrorists

The terrorists, who were now on their own turf in the Libya of militant leader Muammar Qaddafi, ordered that the plane be fueled for a flight of at least four hours. The plane's destination was not revealed to the captain, crew, or passengers, but it appeared that it would be a distant one. Only one passenger was fortunate enough to be released at Benghazi. She was pregnant and on her way to her mother's funeral in Manchester, England. After managing to convince a Libyan doctor that she was in danger of miscarrying, she was allowed to deplane and catch a flight for Manchester.

In the very early hours of June 28, 1976, the now 245 passengers found themselves on the ground in East Africa, at Uganda's Entebbe airport. The final destination chosen by the terrorists was soon explained by the appearance of the Ugandan dictator Idi Amin and a guard of armed Ugandan soldiers. General Idi Amin Dada had overthrown the former government of Uganda in 1971, expelled all Israelis, and broken off relations with Israel in 1972. He then allied himself with Libya and other

Muslim nations hostile to Israel. These developments explained his support of the PFLP.

The passengers were taken from the airplane and herded into an old terminal building, where Israelis and other Jews were separated from the French crew and the rest of the passengers. The real intent of the hijacking now became clear. If the Israeli government did not release some 53 convicted terrorist prisoners from its jails, the 106 Jews held hostage would be executed within 48 hours.

While the Israeli authorities gave the appearance of negotiating with the terrorists, they were busy planning a bold rescue mission known as Operation Jonathan. It was led by Lieutenant Colonel Jonathan Netanyahu, the brother of Benjamin Netanyahu, who later served as prime minister of Israel. The plan was to send a group of long-range aircraft to Entebbe by the extended hostage-execution deadline of July 4, 1976. The planes would be equipped with more than 200 well-armed troops, fully prepared for heavy fighting. Another plane would be on standby to evacuate the hostages, and a hospital aircraft would await any casualties in nearby Kenya.

Operation Jonathan began on July 3, with the Israeli transports arriving at Entebbe airport late that night, after nearly eight hours of flying time. Early the next morning, in a swift ground strike that had been totally unexpected, the Israeli commandos freed the hostages and killed the four original terrorists, as well as several others who had joined the attackers in Libya. In less than one hour, the transports were on their way back to Israel. Only four of the 106 Israeli and other Jewish hostages did not survive the rescue mission. There was also one death among the rescuers, that of the leader of the operation, Jonathan Netanyahu.

The success of the Entebbe rescue operation was due to the Israelis' strategic planning, based on familiarity with the layout of the airport and its defenses. It was also due to the surprise element of the mission and to the ineptness of the Ugandan forces under the command of their leader, Idi Amin.

The failure, however, of the hijackers of Air France Flight 139 did not deter terrorists from attempting similar operations throughout the 1970s and 1980s. Most sky-jackings of that period were aimed at taking large numbers of innocent passengers hostage in order to bargain for the release of terrorists who were being held in Israeli prisons. Also, because of the continued support of Israel by the United States, the Muslim attackers targeted American passengers and airlines in particular.

One of the most prolonged and publicity-directed sky-jackings of the 1980s was that of TWA Flight 847, which began on June 14, 1985, during the Athens-Rome leg of a flight that had just left Cairo, Egypt. In Cairo, a Boeing 727 had been boarded by two Lebanese terrorists, who managed to smuggle two grenades and a pistol past the airport security machines by wrapping them in fiberglass, which at that time served as effective insulation.

The terrorists were members of Islamic Jihad, an extremist group of Shi'ite Muslims living in Lebanon. The majority of the world's Muslims belong to the Sunni branch of the religion. The Shi'ite Muslims, or Shi'a, who make up only 15 percent of the world's Muslims, differ from the Sunni mainly on the question of the rightful successors of Muhammad, the founder of Islam. As militants, however, the Sunni and the Shi'a have been united in their respective struggle against Israel and the United States.

The TWA hijacking of June 14, 1985, began less than

twenty minutes after the plane took off from Athens en route to Rome. More than 100 of the 153 passengers on board were Americans, many of whom were planning to transfer in Rome for a flight to the United States. The American pilot, Captain John Testrake, was ordered at gunpoint to fly the aircraft to Beirut, Lebanon, pending a response to the terrorists' demand for the release of 766 Shi'ite Muslims who were being held in Israeli prisons.

At Beirut, the plane was refueled and nineteen women and children were allowed to leave via an escape chute. It was learned from the freed hostages that the hijackers were beating passengers and hysteria had resulted.

TWA 847 next flew to Algiers, where it remained on the runway for five hours, and twenty-one more passengers were released. As the hijackers' demands were still far from being met, they ordered the plane to return to Beirut. By this time, passports had been collected and Israeli and American males had been singled out for pistol-whipping and other harsh physical treatment. During the return flight to Beirut, Robert Stethem, a young United States Navy diver, was beaten and shot to death. On landing, his body was thrown out of the plane onto the tarmac.

While the world watched in horror on television screens and listened to frequent news flashes on the radio, the plane continued to bounce back and forth between Beirut and Algiers. It was learned that the Israeli passengers had been taken off at Beirut and spirited away, that the two hijackers on board had been joined by additional Shi'ite terrorists, that Captain Testrake had a gun to his head, and that the terrorists were threatening to blow up the aircraft.

The standoff continued for seventeen days, during which time all but thirty-nine American men were taken off the plane. It finally ended on June 30, 1985, with the release of a partial number of Shi'ite prisoners, the freeing of the last of the hostages, and the escape of the terrorists. The Israeli passengers held in Beirut were rescued by special U.S. military antiterrorist units. The response of the American media to the crisis included not only hourly reporting, but interviews with the hostages who had been released during the standoff. The networks competed feverishly for what *The Washington Post* called a "race for on-the-air scoops, making it seem that the hijackers rather than the broadcasters had taken control of the airwaves and were running the show."

The media response to the hijacking of TWA 847 by Islamic Jihad appeared to have encouraged yet another group, the Palestinian Liberation Front (PLF), to utilize another form of public transport for one of its next operations. (The PLF was a small faction of the Palestine Liberation Organization, or PLO.) The *Achille Lauro* was an Italian cruise ship that sailed from Italy in October 1985 for ports of call in Egypt and Israel. On October 7, the ship docked in Alexandria, Egypt. While most of the passengers went ashore on sightseeing trips, four Palestinian terrorists posing as tourists boarded the vessel.

Information later revealed that the terrorists had planned to use the ship as a means of approaching the Israeli port of Ashdod, where they were scheduled to attack several targets on shore. However, after the passengers returned to the ship and it set sail for Egypt's Port Said, a steward discovered that there were guns and ammunition in the newcomers' luggage.

The terrorists then took control of the 427 passengers and 80 members of the crew, firing weapons and collecting passports. They shuffled the American passports and declared that the owner of whichever one came out on top would be their first victim. The topmost passport belonged to Leon Klinghoffer, a sixty-nine-year-old American in a wheelchair. Klinghoffer was shot in the head and killed instantly. Other passengers were ordered at gunpoint to throw his body into the sea. One of the terrorists then sent a radio message to ground headquarters in Tartus, Syria: "We threw the first body into the water after shooting him in the head. Minutes from now we will follow up with the second one. Do not worry, Tartus. We have a lot of them here."

The terrorists then demanded that fifty Palestinians imprisoned in Israel be released and ordered the captain to sail the ship to the port of Tartus. Yasir Arafat, the leader of the PLO felt, however, that the PLF had gone too far, and he instructed Abu Abbas—the PLF mastermind of the botched *Achille Lauro* operation—to negotiate for the surrender of the four terrorists at Port Said.

Abbas, who had not been aboard the ship himself, delivered the four terrorists who were tried in Italy and convicted. The longest sentence, that of Leon Klinghoffer's murderer, was thirty years. Abu Abbas arranged with the Italian authorities to fly him to Sicily, from which he managed to escape. He was finally captured in Baghdad, Iraq, in April 2003. In an interview that Abbas gave to NBC Nightly News television on May 5, 1986, he denied that his PLF foot soldiers had committed an atrocity. "What is the use of killing an old man anyway?" Abbas remarked. "I do not believe our comrades on the boat carried out any killing."

The network was accused of having given voice to a spokesperson for terrorism and a wanted criminal. But it defended itself, stating that it was exercising the privileges of a free press and accommodating the public's right to know.

The largest loss of life in a single air disaster on an

THE REMAINS OF PAN AM 103, WHICH WAS DOWNED BY LIBYAN TERRORISTS OVER LOCKERBIE, SCOTLAND, ON DECMBER 21, 1988, WITH A DEATH TOLL OF 270.

American plane targeted by terrorists took place on December 21, 1988. The flight was the now historic Pan Am 103, a Boeing 747, bound from London's Heathrow Airport for New York.

On board were 259 passengers and crew, of whom 189 were Americans. The Christmas holidays were approaching, and the flight carried a number of American students who had been studying abroad as well as other homeward-bound travelers, plus many British and European visitors en route to the United States.

None reached their destination. As the aircraft approached an altitude of 31,000 feet (9,449 m) on its northerly transatlantic route, it was rocked by a tremendous explosion and crashed over the Scottish town of Lockerbie. Eleven people on the ground were killed, bringing the death toll to 270.

Investigations as to the cause of the crash were extensive.

They finally revealed that a time bomb made out of plastic explosives had been placed aboard the plane in a suitcase, apparently by terrorists who had themselves not boarded the aircraft. Theories as to the identity of the terrorists abounded. They included Palestinian terrorist leader Ahmed Jabril, who had the backing of Syria, as well as that of Iran and Libya, two other states that were known to be sponsors of terrorism.

On November 13, 1991, a federal grand jury in Washington, D.C., indicted two Libyan intelligence officers in absentia. It had evidence that the downing of Pan Am 103 was in retaliation for two United States air strikes against Libya in 1986, following Libya's bombing of a Berlin discotheque frequented by American service personnel, which killed two soldiers and injured more than two hundred people. (Fifty-nine were Americans.)

Years passed, however, before Libya was forced to hand over the accused murderers in the case of Pan Am 103. The United States and Britain obtained Libya's cooperation through United Nations-imposed sanctions on the North African nation ruled by Muammar Qaddafi. The sanctions, which were intended to weaken Libya economically and politically, included cuts in arms sales and oil-related equipment, reduction of air and trade links, and the freezing of Libyan assets abroad.

In April 1999, the two Libyan suspects—Abdel Basset al-Megrahi and Al-Amin Khalifa Fahima—were finally handed over to a Scottish court to be tried on neutral ground in the Netherlands. In January 2001, after a trial lasting nine months, a panel of three judges found al-Megrahi guilty of having planted the bomb that blew up the plane. Fahima, however, was acquitted.

The fifty-year-old al-Megrahi filed an appeal against his conviction, but lost. On March 14, 2002, he was transferred from the Netherlands to a prison in Glasgow, Scotland, to serve out a life sentence with the possibility of parole after twenty years.

Reactions to the conviction and sentence were varied. Senator Edward M. Kennedy, speaking on the floor of the U.S. Senate on March 14, 2002, expressed satisfaction that the verdict against al-Megrahi had been upheld, stating: "Today, after more than thirteen years, a measure of justice has finally been achieved." But he warned that the United Nations Security Council sanctions would not be lifted until the Libyan government accepted full responsibility for the bombing and paid appropriate compensation in the form of reparations to the families of the victims.

Among the victims' families, other government officials, and legal experts who had been following the case there were numerous expressions of dissatisfaction with its outcome. Many unanswered questions remained. Who was responsible for the airport security lapse by means of which the suitcase had been placed on the flight? Was it possible that al-Megrahi had no accomplices? How could a single individual have planned and executed an attack that had such devastating consequences? Finally, assuming that al-Megrahi qualified for parole, was twenty years in jail adequate punishment for the murder of 270 people?

Two factors regarding the downing of Pan Am 103 did appear to be clear. The United States had been the target of a terrorist attack. And Libya's support and sheltering of the accused bombers marked it as a country that practiced state-sponsored terrorism.

7
Sponsored by the State

Libya, Syria, and Iran are Middle Eastern states that have ranked high among those nations with a history of government-sponsored terrorism. Libya's ruler Colonel Muammar Qadddafi came on the scene in 1972, with his support of the Palestinian terrorists' murder of the Israeli athletes at the Munich Olympics. Qaddafi acted once again in 1981 when he sponsored the assassination of Egyptian president Anwar el-Sadat, in retaliation for Sadat's peace efforts toward Israel.

On April 5, 1986, Libya directly attacked Americans with its bombing of the La Belle discotheque in West Berlin, Germany, where many American service personnel were known to spend their leisure time. The death of two American soldiers and the wounding of scores more drew a vigorous response from the United States. On April 15, 1986, the Libyan cities of Tripoli and Benghazi were attacked by one hundred carrier- and land-based U.S. warplanes and by surface-to-air missiles. Although the targets were intended to be military installations only, thirty-seven Libyan civilians were killed, including a young adopted daughter of Colonel Qaddafi.

The growing hostility between Libya and the United States climaxed on December 21, 1988, with the explosion aboard Pan Am 103. Sanctions imposed by the United Nations and the United States gradually brought Libya, in 1999, to the point of yielding the two wanted terrorists, one of whom was convicted and jailed on March 14, 2002.

On May 29, 2002, it was reported that Libya was at long last proposing to pay reparations to the families of the 270 people killed in the downing of Pan Am 103. The amount of reparations offered was $10 million for each victim, a total of $2.7 billion. But the Libyan offer contained a number of conditions. Libya would pay $4 million per victim when the United Nations lifted its sanctions against that country. It would pay another $4 million when United States sanctions against Libya were lifted. And it would pay the final $2 million when the United States took Libya off its list of states that sponsor terrorism.

Most disturbing with regard to Libya's partial attempt to make amends for the bombing of Pan Am 103 was Colonel Muammar Qaddafi's refusal to admit responsibility for the terrorist operation. He insisted that the reparations offer had no official connection with his government. It was being made by the Libyan business sector.

The Libyan government appeared to have refrained for some years from the direct sponsorship of terrorist operations. However, in the light of increasing Islamic militancy toward the West, the United States felt that Libya might well be harboring and supporting Muslim extremists. As a result, there seemed little likelihood that the United States would, in the foreseeable future, remove Libya from its list of state sponsors of terrorism.

Syria is another Middle Eastern nation that has used its power and influence to aid terrorist operations against the United States and Israel. It has done so chiefly through its support of Muslim extremists in the small adjoining country of Lebanon. Both nations have had common and troublesome borders with Israel.

Two major attacks against Americans were carried out in 1983 in Beirut, the Lebanese capital. The first took place on April 18, when a van carrying a bomb tore through the front portion of the seven-story United States Embassy. Sixty-three people, seventeen of whom were Americans, were killed, as well as the suicide bomber who drove the van. Among the American dead were several officials from the U. S. State Department and the Central Intelligence Agency (CIA). One hundred and twenty persons were injured.

Six months later, on October 23, 1983, another suicide attack against Americans was carried out. This time the target was a U.S. Marines compound in Beirut. Some 300 Marines had been sent to Lebanon as part of a peacekeeping force during a period of dangerous conflict between Israel and its Middle Eastern neighbors.

At 6:22 in the morning, a yellow Mercedes truck carrying a bomb containing 12,000 pounds (5,443 kg) of dynamite crashed through the security perimeter of the Marine barracks, killing 241 United States military personnel. Once again, the driver of the truck was killed as well.

Islamic Jihad, the Lebanon-based Shi'ite Muslim terrorist group, claimed responsibility for both the embassy and the Marine compound attacks.

While the Shi'ite Muslim regime in Iran was known to be highly supportive of Lebanese Shi'ite terrorist organizations such as Islamic Jihad and Hezbollah, Syria too played a role in empowering Lebanon's Islamic militants, for it regarded that small country as a strategic prize in its war against Israel. As recently as 2002, Syria was still abetting the bombardment and shelling of Israel's northern border by Islamic terror groups based in Lebanon.

Iran's state-sponsored terrorism attack struck almost without warning in November 1979, following an Islamic revolution in a country formerly friendly to the United States.

For thirty-seven years, Iran had been led by the Shah, or king, Mohammad Reza Pahlavi—a hereditary ruler with leanings toward the West. Unlike most of its neighbors in the Middle East, Iran is not an Arab nation. Until 1935, it was officially known as Persia. Even today about half of its inhabitants are of Persian extraction and only 3 percent are Arabs. Iran's official language is the Persian tongue, Farsi, although it is written in the Arabic alphabet. While Iran is a Muslim nation, it is close to 90 percent Shi'ite Muslim.

Since 1963, one of Iran's leading Islamic clergymen and a longtime foe of the Pahlavi regime had been forced to live in exile, first in Turkey, then in Iraq, and lastly in France. His name was Ruhollah Khomeini and he held the title of Ayatollah, or religious leader. Khomeini denounced the Shah for a number of reasons. They included his exploitation of the country's oil resources, his costly royal displays, and his dictatorial rule enforced by his secret police force known as SAVAK. Above all, Khomeini condemned the Shah for allowing western influences to overtake Iran and for his betrayal of fundamentalist Islam.

Khomeini had powerful influence, even while in exile, and built up such militancy against the Shah that on January 16, 1979, the Shah was deposed and forced to flee the country. On February 1, 1979, Khomeini returned to Iran and set up a fundamentalist Islamic government. Coeducational classes in schools and universities were forbidden, women were forced to return to fully covering the head and body with the black garment known as the chador, and the Revolutionary Guard roamed the streets arresting citizens whose behavior was deemed improper under Islamic law.

Particularly offensive to Khomeini, in view of the Shah's taking refuge in the United States, was the presence of the United States Embassy in the Iranian capital, Tehran. On November 4, 1979, some 400 Iranians, many self-named "Students in the Path of the Imam," stormed the embassy. Marine guards using tear gas were unable to halt the mob. Sixty-six hostages were taken, of whom thirteen were released. After one additional release, 52 Americans were held for 444 days, or nearly 15 months.

In the period leading up to the hostage-taking and throughout that time, the United States was characterized as "the Great Satan" and threats of "death to America" were voiced everywhere in Iran. The Ayatollah Khomeini declared: "I beg God to cut off the hands of all evil foreigners and all their helpers."

In exchange for the fifty-two hostages, the Ayatollah demanded that the Shah, who was in the United States for medical treatment, be returned to Iran so that "revolutionary justice" could be administered to him. But even

AFTER BEING HELD HOSTAGE BY THE FUNDAMENTALIST ISLAMIC GOVERN-MENT OF IRAN FOR 444 DAYS, FROM NOVEMBER 1979 TO JANUARY 1981, THESE AMERICANS ARE RELEASED AND RETURNED HOME.

after the Shah died of a serious illness in July 1980, the government of Iran continued to hold the Americans captive.

Making the hostages appear in public blindfolded while being jeered at by Iranian mobs, forcing them to read anti-American statements on television, and labeling them "spies" and "vipers"—all suited Khomeini's purpose. He used the hostages to incite anger toward the United States and to fuel Islamic fervor among the Iranian people. These tactics contributed to Khomeini's successful takeover of Iran as both religious and political leader.

The American response to the taking of the hostages was a rescue attempt that was poorly organized. In April

1980, eight helicopters carrying U.S. commando forces were sent to Iran. The military operation failed when the helicopters encountered technical problems, resulting in the deaths of eight service personnel. The release of the hostages did not come about until January 20, 1981, the day that President Jimmy Carter left office and Ronald Reagan was sworn in as the new president.

The hostages had suffered serious traumas as a result of their year and a quarter in captivity. Some managed to keep diaries. Their stories told of being separated into small groups, each cut off from the others. They received no outside news and had very limited opportunities to write to their families or receive mail. Their jailers, most of them students, varied in their treatment of the captives. Some were friendly at times and others were consistently hostile and imposed excessive restrictions. The amateur jailers often let food and other essential supplies run out. Medical care was a serious concern, especially among the older embassy-staff prisoners.

Most difficult for the hostages was the psychological strain. They were blindfolded when taken out of their rooms, even for showers or exercise, they had no way of knowing what their government was doing for them, and they were uncertain of when or even if they would ever be released.

By the time the Ayatollah Khomeini died in June 1989, Iran had been completely transformed into an extremist Islamic nation. Although it elected a secular president in 1997, the real power remained in the hands of Khomeini's successor, the Ayatollah Ali Khamenei.

While the country has now had what are termed "open elections," no one not approved by the religious leadership has been allowed to stand for office. Young people and others who have attempted to organize reform movements favoring a secular democracy have been sub-ject to exile, imprisonment, or death.

On the international front, Iran's hard-line Islamic leadership has been responsible for state-sponsored ter-rorism through its support of such groups as Hezbollah, Islamic Jihad, and Hamas. In January 2002, Israeli authori-ties intercepted a shipment of fifty tons of weapons sent by Iran to the Palestinians, aboard the freighter *Karine A.*

The question of how the United States might encourage the pro-democracy movement in Iran, while keeping a wary eye on the Islamic-militant faction that controls the state's domestic and international policies, has yet to be resolved.

8
Homegrown Terrorists

As opposed to governments that sponsor terrorism against other nations, there are those individuals or groups within nations that terrorize members of their own society. In the United States, the Ku Klux Klan carried out its unrestricted racist crusade against African Americans and their white sympathizers for a hundred years, starting in 1865.

During the 1960s and 1970s, counterculture groups known as the New Left sprang up in Europe and the United States, robbing banks and kidnapping and assassinating citizens and government officials for vaguely formulated political and social ideals.

The 1990s saw another rash of homegrown terror operations that grew out of a variety of attitudes and beliefs. Some operations were motivated by fierce antigovernment views. Others were based on mystical religious credos. In some cases, the two approaches fused into one belief system.

FOLLOWING THE SARIN GAS ATTACK ON THE TOKYO SUBWAY IN 1995, JAPANESE FIREFIGHTERS IN PROTECTIVE GEAR HAD TO BE SENT IN TO CLEAN THE CONTAMINATED CARS.

The world was shocked on March 20, 1995, by the news that packages containing a powerful nerve gas called sarin had been placed at strategic points in Japan's vast Tokyo subway system, sickening some 5,500 riders and killing twelve.

Sarin was known to cause death on inhalation by paralyzing the central nervous system. It was soon discovered that the terrorists had placed eleven packages containing the sarin in a liquid solution on five different subway trains. The packages looked like plastic rubbish bags and, when the terrorists punctured them with the specially sharpened tips of their umbrellas, the sarin leaked out onto the floor.

As the fumes dispersed through the transit system, riders on three subway lines and at fifteen stations staggered toward the outdoors, bleeding from the nose and mouth, coughing uncontrollably, or suffering convulsions. Fortunately, weather conditions were good that day and the air was relatively low in humidity, making breathing easier. Otherwise the terrorists' intention to kill hundreds or even thousands might have been realized.

The subway attack was soon traced to a cultlike group that had been operating in Japan since 1987 and was known as Aum Shinrikyo, meaning Supreme Truth. Its leader, who went by the name of Shoko Asahara, had received visions informing him that the end of the world was approaching. Asahara and his followers, whose numbers were reported to have expanded beyond Japan and into the tens of thousands, believed that catastrophe lay ahead for Japan. The only way to avert disaster was to stockpile chemical and biological weapons that were to be used against the United States and against an international conspiracy of Jews and financiers.

The Tokyo subway attack of March 20 was apparently

launched by Aum Shinrikyo in response to information that it had long been under suspicion and that its headquarters and laboratory were about to be raided. When police entered the cult's compound after the nerve gas attack, they discovered alarming quantities of stockpiled sarin, as well as other nerve gases, mustard gas, and biological warfare agents, including anthrax. The terror group was even believed to have been working on the development of a nuclear device.

In December 1995, Japanese authorities disbanded Aum Shinrikyo, seized its assets, and ordered its leaders to face trial. Asahara and eighteen others were jailed. In 2000, with its numbers sharply reduced, Aum Shinrikyo changed its name to Aleph (the first letter of the Hebrew alphabet). It now claims hundreds of new members. Along with other cults, it is currently being carefully watched by Japan's Public Security Investigation Agency.

America's most notorious homegrown terrorist of the 1990s was the twenty-seven-year-old self-styled antigovernment activist who blew up the Alfred P. Murrah Federal Building in Oklahoma City on April 19, 1995, killing 168 men, women, and children, and injuring 500 others.

Timothy McVeigh did not, in his early adulthood, appear to fit the profile of one who would cold-bloodedly murder his fellow citizens. He grew up in a middle-class family in upstate New York, served in the U.S. Army during the Gulf War, and received the Bronze Star before being discharged. McVeigh did, however, have an abiding interest in guns of all sorts and other weaponry, which he pursued by joining the Michigan Patriots while on a visit to a friend's farm in Decker, Michigan.

The Michigan group was a militia, or paramilitary

organization, that was linked to a national network known as the Christian Patriots. The Christian Patriots were white supremacist, anti-Semitic, and deeply antagonistic to the federal government. They strongly objected to any form of government above the county level.

In the Michigan Patriot militia, McVeigh and his friends underwent survivalist and guerrilla warfare training. McVeigh's antigovernment views had been fueled, in part, by the siege of the Branch Davidian compound in Waco, Texas, nearly two years earlier. The Branch Davidians were a religious cult that was preparing for the end of the world by stockpiling weapons. This illegal activity came to the attention of the federal government. There were also reports that the Davidians' leader, David Koresh, was practicing polygamy and abusing minors.

On February 28, 1993, the Bureau of Alcohol, Tobacco, and Firearms (ATF) attempted to send in agents to investigate the illegal weapons charge, and were forced to lay siege to the compound for fifty-one days. The standoff ended on April 19, when a fire broke out and killed about eighty Branch Davidians, including Koresh.

Exactly two years later, on April 19, 1995, Timothy McVeigh drove a truck containing a powerful bomb to the Murrah Federal Building in Oklahoma City, parking it near the building's ATF offices. The offices were located near the day-care center, which was filled in the early morning hours with the children of employees.

The detonation of the bomb sheared away nearly half of the nineteen-story building. Among the dead were nineteen children who were in the day-care center. A little more than an hour after the explosion, McVeigh was apprehended driving a car in which he was carrying a concealed pistol and a knife. His arrest and trial resulted in a conviction for the bombing of the federal building and a death sentence, which was carried out on June 11, 2001.

McVeigh's statements during his imprisonment and trial confirmed the ruthlessness of his intent. When he was asked why he could not have bombed the federal building at night, thus sparing the lives of its daytime occupants, he replied, "We needed a body count to make our point." Timothy McVeigh, the homegrown terrorist, had been responsible for one of the deadliest attacks ever to take place on American soil.

A nervous nation was alarmed a little more than a year later, when a pipe bomb exploded on July 27, 1996, at Atlanta, Georgia's, Centennial Olympic Park during the summer Olympic Games. One person was killed and 112 were injured.

A suspect was arrested but later released. The true perpetrator of the terrorist act appeared to have been an individual named Eric Robert Rudolph. Rudolph, however, had remained at large and gone on to bomb abortion clinics and gay and Lesbian bars in Georgia and Alabama in 1997 and 1998. He was identified as the Olympic Park terrorist when authorities found traces of the same explosive used in Atlanta in his truck and in his storage locker, following his 1998 bombing of a women's health clinic in Birmingham, Alabama.

Rudolph was placed on the FBI's Ten Most Wanted fugitive list. He remained at large for five years and was finally apprehended in May 2003 in the mountainous regions of western North Carolina.

Right-wing conspirators, members of religious cults, antigay and antiabortion activists, and people who are at war with the federal government appear to make up a majority of America's homegrown terrorists. They devise acts of violence intended to kill or injure as many ordinary citizens as possible in order to make a statement or send a message.

Sometimes their motives are less than clear-cut. Such individuals appear to belong to no particular category and may not even bear a grudge. But their actions can be just as potentially lethal as those of terrorists with a marked agenda.

In May 2002, a series of six-inch pipe bombs were discovered in rural home mailboxes in Illinois, Iowa, Nebraska, Colorado, and Texas over a five-day period. The devices were rigged to go off when the flap of the mailbox was lifted, thus endangering the lives of both postal deliverers and homeowners. Of the total of eighteen bombs planted, six went off, causing injuries to four postal workers and two customers.

The homegrown terrorist turned out to be a twenty-one-year-old University of Wisconsin student from Minnesota named Luke John Helder. At his parents' urging, he soon gave himself up. Americans learned that there are about 1,500 pipe bombs planted in the United States each year, and that Helder's crime was essentially of a copycat nature. But what was his reason for planting the bombs?

In a letter that Helder sent to his student newspaper, *The Badger Herald*, on May 3, 2002—the day the first mailbox bomb was discovered—he wrote a long, rambling explanation of his reason for attempting to murder innocent people. The main thrust of his message was that death is not to be feared and that "paradise awaits!" Therefore, Helder concluded, "I'm dismissing a few individuals from reality, to change all of you for the better, surely you can understand my logic." Helder also expressed his distrust of government, warning against its control of its citizens.

Although Helder appeared to have had little contact

with Islam, the question arose as to whether he had been influenced through the media by the approach of a Muslim martyr to death. Also, the television and press publicity given to Helder's crime inspired a rash of pipe bombs being planted around the country in the days that followed.

Helder was officially charged May 10, 2002, on two counts: using an explosive to maliciously destroy property and affect interstate commerce, and using a destructive device to commit a crime of violence that resulted in the wounding of a Tipton, Iowa, woman. If convicted on the first count, he could go to prison for forty years; if on the second count, for life.

9
Osama bin Laden's Network of Terror

The attacks of September 11, 2001, on the World Trade Center and the Pentagon familiarized every American with the name Osama bin Laden. Operations connected with or masterminded by bin Laden had, however, been taking place for a number of years.

Who was bin Laden and what were his motives for targeting American lives and property? Osama was one of more than fifty offspring of a billionaire father who was born in Yemen, moved to Saudi Arabia, and struck it rich as a contractor, building roads, airports, mosques, and palaces for the wealthy ruling house of al-Saud.

Like many of his male siblings, Osama, who was born in 1957 in Saudi Arabia, was raised and educated to become a businessman. But at the onset of the Gulf War, in 1990, he became obsessed with the presence of American troops on Saudi soil.

The Gulf War began on August 2, 1990, as the result of Iraq's invasion, under President Saddam Hussein, of its oil-rich neighbor Kuwait. The United States immediately came to the aid of Kuwait. In order to protect Saudi Arabia from possible invasion as well, the first of some 5,000 American troops were stationed there, starting on August 7, 1990.

Although the Gulf War ended in 1991, the Americans remained in Saudi Arabia, mainly for the purpose of training Saudi troops. Bin Laden, whose religious faith was deep, railed against the presence of the "infidel," or non-Muslims, and declared that the foreigners must be expelled from Saudi Arabia, the land that had been the birthplace of Islam in C.E. 622 and that was home to the two holiest cities of the Islamic faith, Mecca and Medina.

In 1991, in an act of protest against the Saudi government, Osama bin Laden moved his family and his business interests out of Saudi Arabia. He lived for a time in the Sudan and then moved his site of operations to Afghanistan where he had already built roads and other installations with his own fortune and set up training camps for Islamic militants. In Afghanistan, bin Laden was well protected by the presence of the Taliban, the successors to the fierce Islamic fighters who had driven out the Russians in 1989, thus ending the Soviet Union's ten-year occupation of that country. As Taliban control of Afghanistan grew, so did the strength and reach of Osama bin Laden's Al Qaeda terror network. Soon it would begin to unleash itself on the "world leader" that bin Laden sought to destroy.

On a chilly Friday morning, February 26, 1993, a van containing a 1,500-pound (680-kg) bomb was driven into the underground parking garage of New York City's World Trade Center. At 12:18 P.M., lunch hour, a tremendous blast issued from the garage area. The explosion left a crater approximately 150 feet (46 m) in diameter and destroyed five floors of concrete construction, flattening cars in the garage and collapsing support pillars. Systems throughout the buildings were immediately disrupted. Water pipes burst, and electrical lines went out. Elevators were stranded between floors, and office workers were forced to feel their way down darkened stairwells through thick, black smoke. Other occupants clambered up flights of stairs to the observation deck of Two World Trade Center, the South Tower, where most of the damage had occurred. There, they were rescued by helicopter.

Fire and police crews assisted the injured, who reached the street gasping for air, their mouths and noses smudged with soot. Six people died and a final count of those injured came to 1,042. The nation was shocked. Except for Pearl Harbor, the 1993 World Trade Center bombing was the worst international attack so far on American soil in modern times. It took only days to discover that the attackers had been international terrorists. One member of the group, Mohammad Salameh, returned to the agency from which he had rented the Ryder truck used in the bomb blast. He reported the truck stolen and attempted to collect the security deposit. The FBI obtained further proof of his guilt when they discovered traces of the chemicals used in the bomb on the rental contract itself.

Salameh and several other conspirators went on trial in October 1993. All were given life sentences to be served in prisons in the United States. It took two more years to find the leader of the operation, Ramzi Ahmed Yousef, who had trained in Osama bin Laden's camps in Afghanistan. Yousef had disappeared after the bombing, spent some time in the Philippines, and was finally captured in Pakistan.

On examination of the computer Yousef had been using in his Manila apartment in the Philippines in 1994, several other terrorist schemes were brought to light. It was revealed that he had been planning to blow up nearly a dozen American passenger jets, to assassinate Pope John Paul II, and to crash a plane into CIA headquarters in Virginia. His computer also showed evidence of ongoing contact with Osama bin Laden and Al Qaeda.

On January 8, 1998, Ramzi Ahmed Yousef was sentenced to life imprisonment without parole. In plotting the 1993 bombing, Yousef had hoped to take many more American lives and even, perhaps, to topple the World Trade Center towers. In 1995, as he was being flown by helicopter over the towers to a jail cell in Manhattan, one of Yousef's federal guards pointed out to him that the towers were still standing. Aptly foretelling their ultimate destruction, Yousef replied, "They wouldn't be if I had enough money and explosives."

Osama bin Laden remained deeply hostile to the continuing American military presence in Saudi Arabia. During the mid-1990s, he showed his hand in two bombings of American military installations in that country. The city of Riyadh was the site of a school run by the U. S. Army for the purpose of training the Saudi National Guard. At noon, on Friday, November 13, 1995—a time when most Muslims at the training center would be at prayers in the mosque—two car bombs exploded at the center. Most of the American service

OSAMA BIN LADEN, ISLAMIC TERRORIST AND SWORN ENEMY OF THE UNITED STATES, IN AN UNDATED PHOTO WITH A MAP OF THE ARABIAN GULF IN THE BACKGROUND; THE MARKED ITEMS ARE BELIEVED TO BE THE POSITIONS OF AMERICAN MILITARY VESSELS.

personnel were eating lunch there at the time. Seven people were killed, including five Americans. Forty-two were wounded, most of them Americans.

The FBI immediately sent agents to Saudi Arabia to find out who had been responsible for the murders. But even before the agents arrived, the Saudi government arrested four suspects and had them beheaded. Nevertheless, the terror trail soon led to Osama bin Laden, who had directed the operation through his Al Qaeda network.

A much more destructive bombing of an American installation in Saudi Arabia took place the following year, on June 25, 1996. The target this time was the high-rise apartment complex in Dhahran, known as Khobar Towers, which housed American military personnel.

The bomb used in the Khobar Towers disaster was even more powerful than the explosive device that the homegrown terrorist Timothy McVeigh had used to demolish the federal building in Oklahoma City in April of 1995. Like McVeigh, the bombers had parked a truck close to the building and then driven away in a waiting vehicle. The blast caused the entire front of the housing tower to collapse and left a crater filled with rubble. Dozens were killed, including nineteen American service personnel. Two hundred forty Americans were injured. The Saudis pointed to Iranian terrorists as responsible for the Khobar Towers disaster. But it appears in retrospect that both operations in Saudi Arabia may have been bin Laden's, and were intended not only to send a message to the United States, but to destabilize the royal House of al-Saud because of what he perceived as its betrayal of Islam.

Bin Laden now began to make a series of open declarations of what he termed war against the United States. His first lengthy public manifesto was delivered in August

1996. In it he condemned the United States not only for its military presence in Saudi Arabia but for its support of Israel, its bombing of Iraq following the formal conclusion of the Gulf War, and its friendship with the governments of Egypt and Saudi Arabia.

On May 12, 1997, CNN and foreign networks broadcast an interview with bin Laden that had been taped in a hut in the mountains of Afghanistan. Bin Laden's interviewers, journalists Peter L. Bergen and Peter Arnett, had been driven to the secret meeting place at night. In a long-running commentary, the bearded and turbaned six-foot-tall bin Laden, said, "Due to its subordination to the Jews, the arrogance and haughtiness of the U.S. regime [and] other acts of aggression and injustice, we have declared jihad against the U.S., because in our religion it is our duty." In an admission of responsibility for the 1995 and 1996 attacks on Americans in Saudi Arabia, he remarked, "We have focused our attention on striking at the soldiers in the country of the Two Holy Places [Mecca and Medina]."

On May 28, 1998, in an interview with John Miller of ABC News, bin Laden further denigrated the "leader of the new world order" [the United States] and its military. "We have seen in the last decade," he asserted, "the decline of the American government and the weakness of the American soldier."

Bin Laden also made clear his intentions toward American civilians, as both past and future victims of terrorism. "We do not have to differentiate between those dressed in military uniforms and civilians," he stated. "They are all targets."

Bin Laden was now ready to turn his attention to American diplomatic personnel on a major scale. On

August 7, 1998, massive explosions took place simultaneously at two American embassies in East Africa, one in Nairobi, Kenya, and the other in Dar es Salaam, Tanzania.

Once again, the terrorists chose a Friday, the Islamic holy day, when most Muslims employed in the embassies would be at prayers at the mosques. Although the two embassies were 450 miles apart, both bombings were timed to go off at approximately 10:40 A.M. The United States Embassy in Kenya suffered the greater damage, as the bombers in the suicide operation (one of whom survived) were able to drive the truck containing 1,800 pounds (816 kg) of explosives closer to the building. As a result, more than 5,000 people were injured and 213 were killed, most of them Kenyans who either worked at the embassy or were in the vicinity of the blast. Twelve Americans died. In Tanzania, where the bomb, which was stored in a refrigerator truck, went off before coming within close reach of its target, eighty-six were injured and eleven died. All of those who died were Tanzanians.

The surviving terrorists were soon apprehended. All of them had been trained by Al Qaeda and were operating under Osama bin Laden's newly named World Islamic Front for Holy War Against Jews and Crusaders. From Mohammed Odeh, who had been involved in the planning of the Kenya attack, it was learned that several years had gone into the preparation for the dual operation. Sleepers had been sent to both African countries to pave the way for the arrival of the bombmakers and for the establishment of safe houses in which the explosives could be stored and communications with bin Laden maintained.

On August 20, 1998, in response to the embassy attacks of August 7, President Bill Clinton ordered missiles fired from warships in the Red and Arabian Seas as retaliatory strikes. One strike was aimed at a training camp in Afghanistan where bin Laden and his people were said to be having a high-level meeting with other terrorist groups. Although some twenty Afghans were killed, no leadership figures appeared to have been present at the site. The second target was a pharmaceutical plant in the Sudan, which was believed to have backing from bin Laden and to be producing a deadly nerve gas. Although the plant was demolished, proof of the presence of chemical weapons was never found. Safely hidden in the mountainous terrain of Taliban-controlled Afghanistan, Osama bin Laden was planning one more foray against the United States before the attack on American soil of September 11, 2001.

For several years, it had been the practice of American naval ships to refuel in the Yemeni port of Aden, at the tip of the Arabian Peninsula. On the morning of October 12, 2000, as the United States destroyer *Cole* lay offshore being refueled, a small fiberglass boat set out from a beach near the port, heading in the direction of the destroyer. As the skiff approached the end of its fifteen-minute journey to the *Cole*, its two occupants stood and waved a friendly greeting to those on board the American vessel.

Moments later the 500 to 700 pounds (227 to 318 kg) of explosives that had been loaded onto the tiny craft were detonated by its suicide bombers. It smashed into the destroyer's steel hull, tearing a hole approximately 40 by 60 feet (12 by 18 m). Seventeen American sailors were killed and thirty-nine were injured. The damage to the *Cole* was estimated at up to $170 million.

The FBI immediately sent agents to Yemen, where their investigations were hampered by diplomatic roadblocks. When the operational leader of the *Cole* bombing was tracked down, however, he was found to be an affiliate of Osama bin Laden. Not long afterward, bin Laden spoke glowingly of the *Cole* attack in a 2001 Al Qaeda recruitment video. "The heads of the unbelievers," he declared, "flew in all directions, and their limbs were scattered. The victory of Islam had come . . ."

Already the attacks on New York City and Washington, D.C., were in the advanced planning stage. Before the year 2001 ended, the United States felt the full wrath of the terror network of Osama bin Laden.

ON SEPTEMBER 11, 2002, ONE YEAR AFTER THE ATTACK ON THE WORLD TRADE CENTER IN NEW YORK CITY, THOUSANDS GATHERED AT THE SITE TO MOURN THOSE WHO WERE LOST. THE NAMES OF THE DEAD, WHICH AT THAT TIME NUMBERED 2,801, WERE READ ALOUD IN A TWO AND ONE HALF HOUR ROLL CALL.

10

A World Held Hostage

On May 30, 2002—the traditional date of Memorial Day, honoring those Americans who died in the nation's wars— a simple, twenty-minute closing ceremony took place on the sixteen-acre site where New York City's World Trade Center towers once stood.

In just under nine months since September 11, round-the-clock work crews had removed 1.6 million tons of debris from the site, which had become known as Ground Zero. The rubble, however, which had already yielded more than 19,000 body parts and some 50,000 personal items, continued to be sifted through at a landfill on Staten Island [the New York City borough of Richmond] for another six weeks, until July 15, 2002.

The number of people killed in the bombing of the two

110-story buildings, including those in the two hijacked airplanes, was given on that date as 2,823, of whom less than half—only about 1,200—had so far been identified. The dead included 343 New York City firefighters, 37 Port Authority police officers, and 23 New York City police officers, rescue personnel who had rushed into the towers to try to save lives.

In honor of the more than 1,600 unidentified dead, an empty stretcher draped with an American flag was carried across the bare field. Only the sounds of fire bells, drums, and bagpipes, and the playing of taps marked the ceremony, which began at 10:29 in the morning, the exact time when the North Tower, the second of the two, collapsed.

The complete September 11 death toll was, of course, larger than the World Trade Center count. The Pentagon bombing had claimed 184 lives, both on the ground and on the hijacked plane used for the attack. Also, 40 people died on the plane that had been diverted from its probable target in Washington, D.C., and that crashed in a field in western Pennsylvania. As a result, the September 11 attack was calculated to have taken 3,047 lives. The 19 hijackers who were killed in the terror operation were not included in the final death count.

One of the things that became evident after September 2001 was that the number of deaths, per international terror incident, had been increasing since the 1970s. The murder in 1972 of eleven Israeli athletes in Munich by the Black September group was surpassed in the 1980s and 1990s by events that took lives in the hundreds rather than the tens. Those operations included the 1983 attack on the U.S. Marine barracks in Beirut, Lebanon (241 lives), the 1988 bombing of Pan Am 103

(270 lives), and the 1998 United States Embassy bombings in Kenya and Tanzania (224 lives).

Would the 2001 attack on New York City and Washington, D.C., with more than 3,000 killed, foreshadow larger and larger death tolls? The terrorist threats of the twenty-first century pointed increasingly toward the deployment of chemical, biological, radiological, and nuclear (CBRN) weapons of mass destruction. The potential use of chemical agents such as nerve gases, of biological weapons such as anthrax and smallpox, of radioactive bombs, and of nuclear devices loomed over a world already held hostage by terrorism. Would the unleashing of CBRNs lead to death counts in the tens of thousands or even hundreds of thousands?

It also became evident after 2001 that the nation being singled out for the boldest and most deadly attacks on civilians was the United States. The targeting of the United States appeared to be related to its position as the world's only superpower. With its broad economic, cultural, and military influence, and its sometime lack of sensitivity to the complex outlooks of other cultures and societies, America had come to be seen as the enemy by actual and would-be international terrorists.

In spite of its strengths, the United States is a highly vulnerable target. It is a democracy and a large, open society that values civil rights and individual liberties. It has the world's longest undefended border, with Canada, and a 2,000-mile (3,219-km) porous boundary with Mexico. In dealing with radical fundamentalist Islam, it may imprison convicted terrorists, such as the perpetrators of the 1993 World Trade Center bombing. But it has no judicial weapon against terrorists who choose suicide, as did the bombers who brought down the twin towers in 2001.

Why Is Terrorism Increasing?

A review of terrorist operations and activities over the past century reveals the many faces of terrorism. Violence has erupted as a result of racism, economic distress, leftist and rightist political ideologies, nationalist aspirations and demands, and religious extremism.

Today, the last two—as illustrated by the Palestinian-Israeli conflict and the attacks against the West by Islamic fundamentalists—appear to dominate the struggle, with the latter having the most impact on the international scene.

Bernard Lewis, author of *What Went Wrong: Western Impact and Middle Eastern Response*, wrote in *The New Yorker* on November 19, 2001: "For bin Laden and those who follow him, this is a religious war, a war for Islam and against infidels, and therefore, inevitably, against the United States, the greatest power in the world of the infidels."

Following a lengthy discussion of Muslim antagonism toward the West and its history, Lewis concludes that, "If bin Laden can persuade the world of Islam to accept his views and his leadership, then a long and bitter struggle lies ahead."

Other writers have similarly forecast that terrorism by Muslim extremists against the West, and especially the United States, is bound to increase in the coming years. Among the reasons for continuing conflict are: the position of the United

States as the world's single major power, a position almost un-precedented in history, making it the principal global target; and the combination of religious fervor, national alliances, and use of modern technology among Muslim extremists.

Madeleine K. Albright, United Nations ambassador and secretary of state from 1993 to 2001, analyzed the only-partial success the United States had had so far in the war against terrorism. In *The New York Times* on September 13, 2002, she wrote:

During the past four years, Al Qaeda has attacked Ameri-cans here at home, in Africa and in the Middle East. We still do not know where its top operatives are or what they might be planning. There is evidence that Qaeda members are re-turning to Afghanistan, where thousands of Taliban support-ers live and lawlessness prevails.

We have not given the government of Hamid Karzai even a fraction of the help it needs to make Afghanistan a perma-nent terrorist-free zone. Creation of an effective worldwide antiterror coalition remains a work in progress. Restructur-ing our intelligence services, law enforcement agencies and military to defeat the terrorist threat continues to be in the design stage.

Through the eyes of the experts, we are thus given some of the reasons why terrorism is increasing and may continue to do so in the future.

Terrorist cells around the world are in communication with their headquarters through the Internet and high-speed phone connections. They use videotapes, chat rooms, and Web sites to recruit and mobilize adherents to their cause. As a result, it is estimated that at least 10,000—and perhaps as many as 50,000—Islamic terrorists are distributed in more than fifty countries on five continents.

Another difficulty in fighting terrorism in today's world is the widespread use of technology among terrorist groups. Islamic and other militants have already displayed their use of modern technology for purposes of warfare, and may well employ more sophisticated weapons, such as CBRNs, in the future.

Militant Islam has also made use of modern technology for purposes of communication, propaganda, and publicity. Islamic societies may keep women veiled and prevent their full participation in the life of the community. Islam may maintain strict rules for relationships between the sexes and prohibit open access to television, the press, and other popular media. But the militant groups within these societies make full use of the tools of the information age.

Television networks everywhere have served to portray and publicize the disasters brought about by terrorist operations and to air propaganda by such figures as Osama bin Laden. On October 7, 2001, just weeks after the September 11 attack, the Al Qaeda leader was seen on television issuing the following videotaped warning: "As to America, I say to it and its people a few words: I swear to God that America will not live in peace until peace reigns in Palestine, and not before all the army of infidels depart the land of Mohammed, peace be upon him." [These words preceded by hours the first United States-led assault on the Taliban in Afghanistan.]

What counterterrorism measures can a country like the United States employ to stem the growing menace of deadly premeditated attacks on civilians that may well outdo all past terrorist acts?

Knowing the enemy and maintaining constant vigilance are basic requirements of counterterrorism. For some years, the U.S. government has kept lists of foreign terrorist organizations (FTOs). At present, they number about thirty, including Al Qaeda and, more recently, the Islamic Movement of Uzbekistan (IMU). Similarly, there is a government list of nations that are considered state sponsors of terrorism. The seven countries currently on the list are Iran, Iraq, Libya, Syria, Sudan, North Korea, and Cuba.

In the wake of the September 11 attack, however, the vigilance of the FBI, CIA, and other law enforcement and public security agencies of the government was called into question. It was learned, for example, that in the months prior to the attack, FBI field agents had reported that an unusually large number of Middle Eastern men had been attending flight schools in the United States. Yet, FBI head-quarters in Washington failed to launch an investigation of this phenomenon.

It was also learned that on August 16, 2001, a flight-school enrollee, who was possibly meant to be the twenti-eth of the nineteen hijackers, had been taken into custody in Minnesota. But senior officials of the FBI had refused field agents a warrant to search the suspect's computer, phone records, and other belongings.

On August 21, 2001, there was a terror warning from the CIA to the Immigration and Naturalization Service (INS) and the FBI to be on the lookout for two men suspected of having planned the October 2000 bombing of the destroyer *Cole*. The men, who were already in the country, could not be traced. After the September 11 attack, it was learned that the two suspects had been among the hijackers on the plane that hit the Pentagon.

These instances, plus others, of poor coordination both within and among intelligence-gathering and security agencies led, in the months after the attack, to demands for a reshaping of the government's longtime counter-terrorism arms.

As the nation's premier law enforcement agency, the FBI, in particular, undertook to incorporate a number of changes in its structure and operation. The changes were to include the following: improved communications within the agency; closer and more effective ties with the CIA and other government intelligence agencies; overhauling the bureau's antiquated computer technology and other informational systems; and recruitment of more qualified and better-trained personnel.

Tightening the operations of the FBI and focusing them more directly on counterterrorism appeared to be an important step toward protecting the nation's security. However, increased surveillance of suspected terrorists also raised the specter of violations of civil rights. New security measures might well include surveying worshippers in mosques, making unauthorized searches and seizures of computers and other personal property, and detaining suspects without "probable cause" [convincing proof of reasons for suspicion]. Clearly, one of the effects of terrorism—and of September 11 in particular—was going to be the problem of finding a balance between public security and personal liberty.

Even the more thorough body searches and inspections of carry-on belongings at airports after September 11 raised some citizen objections. Most members of the flying public agreed, however, that in view of the recent use of airplanes as flying bombs, searches and minor disruptions were not an excessive invasion of their individual freedoms.

In June 2002, the administration of President George W. Bush proposed a new, more broad-based approach to the problem of national security in the face of international terrorism. It sought the creation of an agency to be known as the Department of Homeland Security. The FBI and the CIA would continue to operate independently, but would also act in conjunction with the new department, the director of which would be a member of the president's cabinet.

The Department of Homeland Security would incorporate subdivisions of other agencies and departments such as the Coast Guard, immigration, disaster emergency services, and even a bioterrorism sector, adding up to as many as twenty-two different units. As envisioned by the Bush administration, the new department would have 170,000 employees and would cost at least $40 billion a year.

Some legislators viewed the proposed department as too large and bulky to operate effectively, as well as too costly. Others were willing to go along with the proposal in an attempt to shape it into a functional new counterterrorism arm of government.

What weapons, in addition to sharpening its intelligence-gathering capability, can a government employ in its war against terrorism? In the past, victimized nations sometimes sought to bargain with terrorists for the release of hostages. Others refused to negotiate on principle and, as time passed, this policy became widespread.

Attempts at international diplomacy with hostile or rogue nations also proved unsuccessful in most cases. Failure led to efforts to isolate belligerents through embargoes, refusing them the sale of essential economic goods, and persuading other members of the international community to deprive them of military weapons. The imposing of sanctions on Libya by the United Nations and the United

States after the bombing of Pan Am 103 proved partially successful, but only after the passage of many years.

A remaining option was the use of military force against nations or groups responsible for terrorist acts. In the past, the United States had undertaken short-term bombing operations in response to some of the acts of violence against Americans that had taken place abroad. Following the Al Qaeda attack of September 11, 2001, however, there was an immediate resolve to launch a well-mobilized military operation, with the goal of wiping out Al Qaeda and its Taliban hosts in Afghanistan.

On October 7, 2001, President George W. Bush ordered the first strike against the enemy. A massive buildup of fighting ships equipped with cruise missiles and military aircraft launched a long-distance air war over Afghanistan. But the difficulty of hitting designated targets in a land of rugged terrain and secret hideouts immediately became apparent. An estimated 45,000 Taliban fighters, equipped with guns, tanks, aircraft, and anti-aircraft weapons—supplied mainly by Osama bin Laden—were on the ground. Their opponents, the anti-Taliban forces known as the Northern Alliance, numbering 12,000 to 15,000, required both equipment and ground assistance.

By November 2001, supportive air strikes and strategic field operations had enabled the Northern Alliance to move south, resulting in the capture of Kabul, the Afghan capital. In December, Kandahar, another important city, fell to the anti-Taliban forces. American and British ground troops in Afghanistan were soon joined by teams from seventeen nations. Some were assigned to peacekeeping duties in the conquered areas. With much of the country still a war zone, others remained actively engaged in pockets of fighting against the Taliban.

By the summer of 2002, however, neither Osama bin

Laden nor the anticipated number of Taliban fighters or Al Qaeda members had been apprehended. It was believed that the majority of the enemy had slipped over the Afghan border into northwest Pakistan, a wild region over which the Pakistan armed forces had little control.

Meantime, in June 2002, an effort was made to establish a stable government in Afghanistan, which had been without a central administration since its king was exiled in 1973. A traditional grand council, known as a *loya jirga*, convened in Kabul. Sixteen hundred delegates attended. They represented a variety of ethnic groups from all over Afghanistan. Attendees included the native Pashtun clan, Tajiks, Hazaras, and Uzbeks from the north of the country, and local chieftains. The latter were often referred to as warlords because they governed their own regional enclaves and traditionally resisted central rule. The nine-day loya jirga resulted in the election of Hamid Karzai, a Pashtun, who had already served as interim leader of a provisional Afghan government for six months.

President Karzai appointed five vice presidents in an effort to balance his fragile ethnic coalition, and national elections were to be held in two years. Several weeks after the loya jirga's choice of Hamid Karzai, however, one of his appointees—a Pashtun like him—was assassinated. The problem of achieving both an ethnic balance and democratic representation—including women and women's issues—in the new government remained a matter of concern.

There were additional reasons for instability and unrest in Afghanistan. America's retaliatory strike against terrorism had resulted in numbers of civilian deaths. There was also an overwhelming need throughout the country for humanitarian aid in the form of food programs, health services, and the rebuilding of bombed-out homes and villages, especially in the former Taliban-controlled regions.

Will violent and deadly premeditated attacks on civilians and other noncombatants for the purpose of instilling fear and disrupting normal life ever end? The answer is probably not. Some terrorist groups and nations that are today holding the world hostage for the achievement of their political, social, or religious goals may come to realize, as others have in the past, that their acts of terror are self-defeating in the long run, or they may simply be wiped out. But new terrorist causes, seen as justified by their adherents, are almost certain to come to the fore as time goes on.

Terrorism, therefore, is a problem that cannot be solved, but can only be managed. In addition to instituting the most effective surveillance systems and coordinating with the counterterrorism efforts of other nations, what additional measures can be taken to deal with this threat?

A sound foreign policy for a nation as powerful as the United States is an imperative. Such an outlook would call for attention to growing problems in the world's trouble spots and intervention for peace through global coalitions and alliances among the community of nations. Above all, the challenge of the coming years will be for the United States to present itself as a good world neighbor and to try to persuade the anti-democratic forces, by example and by education, to appreciate the benefits of living in a free, fair, and open society.

Notes

Foreword
p. 9, *Newsweek*. September 24, 2001.

Chapter 1
p. 13, Hoffman, Bruce. *Inside Terrorism*.
p. 23, "Inside the Terror Network," *PBS Frontline*. January 17, 2002.

Chapter 2
p. 25, Chalmers, David M. *Hooded Americanism*.
p. 27, Ibid.
p. 28, Nash, Jay Robert. *Terrorism in the 20th Century*.
p. 28, Ibid.
p. 29, Laqueur, Walter. *The Age of Terrorism*.

Chapter 3

p. 40, "Belfast Rioters Attack the Police," *The New York Times*, January 11, 2002.

p. 42, "Haika, the New Basque Separatists," CNN.com, March 6, 2001.

p. 43, "Sri Lanka: Draft Peace Accord," *The New York Times*, February 8, 2002.

Chapter 4

p. 51, Hoffman, Bruce. *Inside Terrorism*.

p. 55, Bodansky, Yossef. *Bin Laden: The Man Who Declared War on America*.

p. 57, Remnick, David. "Rage and Reason," *The New Yorker*, May 6, 2002.

p. 58, Hassan, Nasra. "An Arsenal of Believers," *The New Yorker*, November 19, 2001.

pp. 58–59, Benet, James. "Rash of New Suicide Bombers," *The New York Times*, June 21, 2002.

p. 61, "Shattered Dreams of Peace: The Road From Oslo," *PBS Frontline*, July 2002.

Chapter 5

p. 69, Carassava, Anthee. "Greece Reports First Breakthrough against Terrorist Group," *The New York Times*, July 7, 2002.

pp. 69–70, Carassava, Anthee. "Greeks Claim Victory over Terrorist Group," *The New York Times*, July 19, 2002.

Chapter 6

pp. 78–80, Williams, Louis Maj. (Res.), "Entebbe Diary," Israel Defense Forces.

p. 84, Zacharia, Janine. "*Achille Lauro* Terrorist Chief Not on [FBI] Most-Wanted List," *The Jerusalem Post*, October 12, 2001.

Chapter 7

p. 94, Ode, Robert C. "Excerpts from an Iran Hostage's Diary," Jimmy Carter Library and Museum, October 12, 2001 (last modified).

Chapter 8

p. 99, Larimer, Tom, "Why Japan's Terror Cult Still Has Appeal," *Time*, June 10, 2002.

p. 101, Brooke, James, McVeigh quote, *The New York Times*, March 1, 1997.

Chapter 9

p. 110, Bergen, Peter L. Holy War, Inc.

Chapter 10

p. 119, "A Nation Challenged," *The New York Times*.

p. 121, "Glimmers of Warning: Who Knew What . . ." *The New York Times*, May 17, 2002.

Further Information

Further Reading

Arnold, Terrell E., and Moorhead Kennedy. *Think About Terrorism: The New Warfare.* New York: Walker, 1988.

Greenberg, Keith. *Terrorism: The New Menace.* Brookfield, CT: Millbrook Press, 1994.

Hyde, Margaret O., and Elizabeth H. Forsyth. *Terrorism: A Special Kind of Violence.* New York: Dodd, Mead, 1987.

Meltzer, Milton. *The Truth about the Ku Klux Klan.* New York: Franklin Watts, 1982.

Szumski, Bonnie, ed. *Terrorism, Opposing Viewpoints.* St. Paul, MN: Greenhaven Press, 1986.

Web Sites

www.cia.gov/terrorism

Offers information on United States strategy against terrorism, as well as many publications and reports.

www.terrorismanswers.com
Explanations of United States policy against terrorists.

www.terrorism.com

This site contains original research and documents about terrorism, including profiles of terrorist organizations and counterterrorist groups. It also includes a list of terrorist-related Web pages.

Bibliography

Ansari, Masud. *International Terrorism: Its Causes and How to Control It.* Washington, D.C.: Mas-Press, 1988.

Bergen, Peter L. Holy War, Inc.: *Inside the Secret World of Osama bin Laden.* New York.: Free Press, 2001.

Bodansky, Yossef. *Bin Laden: The Man Who Declared War on America.* Roseville, CA: Prima Publishing, 2001.

Carr, Caleb. *The Lessons of Terror: A History of Warfare against Civilians: Why It Has Always Failed and Why It*

Will Fail Again. New York: Random House, 2002.

Chalmers, David M. *Hooded Americanism.* New York: Franklin Watts, 1976.

Hoffman, Bruce. *Inside Terrorism.* New York: Columbia University Press, 1998.

Laqueur, Walter. *The Age of Terrorism.* Boston: Little, Brown, 1987.

Lewis, Bernard. *What Went Wrong: Western Impact and Middle Eastern Response.* New York: Oxford University Press, 2002.

Long, David E. *The Anatomy of Terrorism.* New York: Free Press, 1990.

Nash, Jay Robert. *Terrorism in the Twentieth Century.* New York: M. Evans, 1998.

The New York Times: A Nation Challenged. New York: The New York Times/Callaway, 2002.

Pillar, Paul R. *Terrorism and U.S. Foreign Policy.* Washington, D.C.: Brookings Institution Press, 2001.

Rashid, Ahmed. *Jihad: The Rise of Militant Islam in Central Asia.* New Haven: Yale University Press, 2002.

Tanner, Raymond. *Rogue Regimes: Terrorism and Proliferation.* New York: St. Martin's Press, 1998.

Index

Page numbers in **boldface** are illustrations.

About the Author

LILA PERL has published more than fifty books for young people and adults, including fiction and nonfiction. Her nonfiction writings have been mainly in the fields of social history, family memoir, and biography. She has traveled extensively to do cultural and background studies of seven African countries, as well as China, Puerto Rico, Guatemala, and Mexico. She has written on subjects as diverse as foods and food customs, genealogy, Egyptian mummies, Latino popular culture, and the Holocaust. Her most recent books for Benchmark Books were *To the Golden Mountain: The Story of the Chinese Who Built the Transcontinental Railroad*

141

and *Behind Barbed Wire: The Story of Japanese-American Internment During World War II.*

Two of her books have been honored with American Library Association Notable awards: *Red-Flannel Hash and Shoo-Fly Pie* and *Four Perfect Pebbles.* Nine titles have been selected as Notable Children's Trade Books in the Field of Social Studies. Lila Perl has also received The Boston Globe Horn Book award, a Sidney Taylor Committee award, and a Young Adults' Choice award from the International Reading Association. The New York Public Library has twice cited her work among Best Books for the Teen Age, most recently in 2003 for *North across the Border: The Story of the Mexican Americans*, published by Benchmark Books.

Lila Perl lives in Beechhurst, New York.